# Why I am

*A Product of the American Dream*

Written By

**Joseph P. Ludovici**

Jo Jo.

I Am so grateful that you Are my son, And that you have grown into such A good young man. I hope you will share this book with your children And Grandchildren so they. I Am proud of you And love you so much!

Dad 2025

# Table of Contents

# Dedication

This book is dedicated to my children, Alexis, Ashlyn, and Joseph Jr. The story is about how their grandparents came from different worlds, but through hard work, education and sacrifice, they accomplished the American Dream. I hope someday they will share this story with their children.

# Acknowledgment

I want to first acknowledge my Parents, Phil and Barbara Ludovici, for without them there would be no story to tell. I want to thank my wife, Lorena, for allowing me to take this journey and especially my amazing trip to Italy in 2023 from which much of this story is drawn. I want to thank my friends Benton Wood and Frank Aguillar for their editorial efforts and encouragement. I want to thank the folks at Amazon KDP Publishing for putting this all together for me and making my dream a reality when I knew very little about this process.

# Prologue

The sterile scent of the hospital filled the air, mingling with the beeping of monitors and the distant murmur of medical staff. Lying in the bed, my chest wrapped in bandages, I felt an unusual heaviness, as though the weight of the world had been laid upon me. It was the spring of 2009, and I found myself staring at the ceiling, my thoughts a whirl of uncertainty and reflection.

With each steady beep of the monitor, my mind wandered to all the untold stories and moments of my life. I began to ponder the idea of capturing these memories, of leaving something behind that could be shared with loved ones. The notion of having a legacy, of preserving my experiences and reflections in a tangible form, felt suddenly urgent.

In the quiet of that hospital room, the seed was planted: what if I could write down these stories? What if I could document my life before it was too late? And so, in those moments of vulnerability, the idea for this book began to take shape.

It was 2009 when I began thinking of writing this book, which, as the scene above explains, was also the time when I had quadruple bypass surgery. I was only forty-five years old and did not know whether I would be around long enough to grow old and tell my kids and grandkids boring stories about my life like old men like to do. This book is about me, the product of the American Dream. I am a fifth-generation Floridian on my maternal grandfather's side and a fourth-generation Floridian on my maternal grandmother's side and This is a rare occurrence in Florida. My "American" side of the family dates back to pre-Revolutionary times in Virginia and North Carolina; I have relatives who fought in both the Revolutionary War and the Civil War. My family had significant wealth prior to the Civil War, after which most of it was lost, thus necessitating the move to Florida.

My paternal grandparents ("Nonni") immigrated to this country from Fiugni, located in the beautiful mountainous region of Abruzzo, Italy. It is a small village that was once a border town of the Papal States where my Nonni were born at the turn of the nineteenth century. My Nonno came to America with fifty-three dollars and he made a very comfortable life for his family through hard work. My mother and father took the opportunities afforded to them through higher education and fulfilled their quest for the American Dream. While the streets of America were not paved with gold as many claimed around the turn of the nineteenth century, hard work and perseverance enabled my four grandparents to lay the foundation upon which my parents built a legacy that will be passed down to my children and grandchildren.

I am very proud of both my Floridian and Italian heritage. In my view, having the chance to work hard and achieve your goals is what America is all about, and I am a product of that fulfilled American Dream. I am not an elite athlete, a business tycoon, a political leader, or a celebrity. There are many memoirs out there by these people. But as Tim Tebow said in *Through My Eyes*, "everyone has a story to tell." I am just a Dad who loves his kids very much and wants them to know where they came from. If you choose to read along with them, I hope you will be entertained, amused and inspired.

# Chapter 1

# My Neighborhood Family

*Dad burst into the hospital room, his face a mix of panic and confusion. "Puddin', I lost my parents!" He exclaimed.*

*Mom, nine months pregnant and already on an emotional rollercoaster, immediately dissolved into tears. Her mind raced to the worst possible scenarios. "Lost?" She gasped, clutching her belly. "What do you mean? Were they in a car accident? Or-oh, God – a plane crash?"*

*Nonni had been visiting Aunt Bea in Philadelphia and were supposed to fly home that day to take care of Ed while Mom prepared for my arrival.*

*Dad froze, bewildered by her reaction. "What's wrong? Why are you crying?"*

*"Your parents," she sobbed, "are they... are they dead?"*

*"What? No!" Dad blurted, now as flustered as ever. "I mean, I literally lost them at the airport! Either they missed their flight, or it got delayed."*

*Mom exhaled sharply, wiping her tears. "Oh, thank God. When you said 'lost,' I thought you meant..." She paused, shaking her head. "Never mind."*

1

**Why I am Who I Am**                    **Joseph P. Ludovici**

*The room, once thick with tension, now seemed almost comical as the misunderstanding unraveled.*

*Perhaps the shock or the crying accelerated the labor, and I was born just a short time later that afternoon.*

### *124th Street*

This is how she (my mom) tells me the conversation went right before I caught my first glimpse of the world on August 20, 1963, at Doctors Hospital in Coral Gables, Florida.

I was born as the second son of Philip Ferdinand and Barbara Ann Hicks Ludovici. My older brother, Ed, was born twenty-three months prior to my birth, meaning he is one month short of being two years older than me. In Miami, we lived in a three-bedroom, one-bath house on Southwest 124th Street just a block west of US 1. Of course, I was too young to remember living at this house, but I have been told that we had a single air conditioner – a window unit – at one end of the long hall.

The one enduring legacy of the house on 124th Street was tacos. Yes, the Mexican dish. Our behind-the-house neighbor was from South Texas and of Mexican descent. She often babysat Ed and made fresh tortillas for him with a tortilla iron. When we left the house on 124th, our neighbor gave my Mom her tortilla iron. From then on, my Mom would make tacos at least once a month, and she still does on special occasions to this day. To do so, you mix white cornmeal with water into a paste, then roll the paste into a small ball about the size of a golf ball and put it on one side of the iron. Next, you fold over the other half of the iron and press down with the leverage arm, which was usually my job. You have to apply the perfect pressure to make the tortilla the ideal thickness. Once done, Mom then fried them in a pan, not in oil, just a bare frying pan, until they were slightly browned—still floppy but cooked. Mom didn't make our tacos with ground beef, as most of us do today. Instead, we used shredded pot roast.

Earlier in the week, we would have Dad's favorite: pot roast with carrots and potatoes. Mom would take the leftover meat and shred it, chop the carrots and potatoes up, and that was our filler. They were awesome and, fitting for a teenager's portion size, Ed could eat probably fifteen, and I was right behind him. As we got older, Mom cooked two roasts, one to eat Monday night and one for tacos later in the week.

## *122ⁿᵈ Street*

When I was two, we moved across the highway to 122$^{nd}$ Street and 77$^{th}$ Avenue, which was then known as unincorporated Dade County, Florida. It is now the Village of Pinecrest, but back then, I always told people I lived in south Miami, meaning not South Miami, the city, but south of there: "Yeah, south of Kendall, no, not Homestead. I will just show you on a map." The house on

122$^{nd}$ Street was an awesome house to grow up in. It was a three-bedroom, two-bathroom ranch style home, and despite the three bedrooms, my brother and I shared a bedroom. It was not a split floor plan, and our room was right next to our parents' room, which, as I got older, made sneaking in or out impossible. Not that I would ever do that.

Given that the lot was a full acre, it gave my parents the opportunity to expand the house several times. The first expansion was a family room behind the dining room. My Mom and Nonno dug most of the foundation by hand with a pick and shovel—no easy task, given the solid coral rock just inches below the topsoil. My Mom wanted her own closet and dressing room, so my dad built her one off the master bedroom with a makeup vanity included. The third major expansion was the new garage. We enclosed the front porch and original garage and converted it into a game room with a beautiful pool table and built a garage big enough to fit three cars when the hurricanes approached. The garage had an open ceiling, and my dad would hang everything from the ceiling rafters on nails. When you needed something down from the rafters, you used a broom handle with a nail through it to unhook the item. Everything you could imagine hung from the rafters.

The garage had a long workbench, and every conceivable tool you needed was hanging either on the plywood-covered wall with nails extruded above the workbench or stowed in holes drilled into a one-by-six that protruded from the wall. My dad worked five and a half days a week as an attorney, and then Saturday afternoons and Sundays after church were spent in his garage. He could do masonry, carpentry, electrical, plumbing, and even mechanical work. I never saw a repairman at my house when I was young, between he and my Nonno, they could fix anything. When we got older, my brother and I would learn a lot of these skills from Dad. My brother enjoyed this much more than I did, and if given a chance after church to either break down and clean a carburetor on the lawn mower in the garage or make pancake batter with my Mom in the kitchen, Ed was in the garage, and I was in the kitchen.

As kids, we had chores, chores, and more chores, it seemed, than the other kids in the neighborhood. We had a monthly chore list filled out on graph paper hanging on the refrigerator containing our daily chores and weekly chores. The daily chores included washing dishes, emptying the dishwasher, taking out the garbage, doing homework, reading, making the bed, putting away clothes, and so on, which, each evening, we would check off the list. On the other hand, the weekly chores included mowing the lawn, weeding the rock garden around the pool (the worst), and vacuuming the pool, allowing us to earn another dollar for the month. After school, we completed our homework and then started on our chores. Only after these were done were we allowed to go outside and play. The list was endless, to be honest, but if we completed our chores for the week, we received an allowance of twenty-five cents for the week.

With our chores done we would head outside. We made up games to play, including one of my favorites, "punting." We had two oak trees in our front yard about 30 yards apart. One player would start at a tree and punt the football to the other player. That player would punt it back, and the game would proceed until you won by catching the ball in front of the other player's tree. I also spent hours just kicking a soccer ball against the back wall of the family room. It was ideal since there were no windows, and you could not hear the ball hitting the wall because of the chimney and hidden closets my dad built. I never played soccer but I could kick a ball pretty well. We also had a basketball hoop over the garage door. It sat on the roof and was supported by braces. Our favorite game was "HORSE." You had to make the other player's shot, or you got a letter. If you got HORSE, you lost. When I got a new basketball for Christmas, I immediately went out to shoot hoops. The ball got stuck on one of the braces, and I tried to get it down with a ladder. Unfortunately, I was not tall enough to climb on the roof and fell off the ladder. My first concussion and a Christmas day spent in a darkened bedroom. Unfortunately, this would be the first of several concussions I would suffer. The worst being in

# Why I am Who I Am                    Joseph P. Ludovici

College when I suffered three days of amnesia after hitting my head while coming down with a pass in flag football.

Ed was invaluable for teaching me important lessons in life. One time, he was teaching me how to shoot a rock out of my nose. The idea was to put a small pebble in one nostril, shut the other nostril with your finger, and then shoot the pebble out by blowing really hard. When I tried, I got the rock too far up my nose. I blew as hard as I could, but it would not come out. My Mom had to take me to the doctor to have it removed. Lesson learned. Another time, Ed taught me how to bite an earthworm in half. When it rained hard, earthworms would wiggle out onto the driveway. Ed showed me how to bite them in half. The only problem was Ed was pulling them apart, not really biting them. A sleight-of-hand trick! I bit it in half with my front teeth. Yes, they taste like dirt. Valuable lesson learned! The last time Ed and I got into a fight (yes, we fought often as kids), he tried to punch me and I blocked the punch. He ruptured a tendon in his ring finger. To this day, it still does not straighten all the way. This time, he learned the lesson. I would end up bigger and stronger than him. This is a good lesson for all older brothers to learn about younger brothers.

Our friend Mark Hoven lived across the street from us. His parents were divorced, and after living in Keys with his Mom, he was able to move back to his Dad's house on the street. His dad was a pilot for National Airlines and then Pan Am. He had a lot of hobbies, including photography, magic, motorcycles, and the coolest was parachuting. He would let us hold the harness around our shoulders as he packed his chute after a jump. He also made the neighborhood kids a pancake breakfast every few months. Mark had a pool, as we did, and many afternoons, we would be swimming in either pool, playing fake professional wrestling or seeing how long we could hold our breath or swim underwater. Mark was amazing; he could swim back and forth six times in one breath. He did not have to hold his nose because he could seal his nose with his upper lip—never knew of anyone else who could do that. As we got older, Mark went to work for my dad. He was involved in all the commercial real estate maintenance and construction Ed, and I did as teenagers and in college. He was also our fraternity brother and was always the one responsible for building our homecoming float. He had amazing design skills and construction skills he learned with us. Like Gibbs on *NCIS*, one of my favorite TV shows, Mark even built a wooden boat for himself in his garage.

The Grays lived next to Mark. Bobby was older and not really in our group. Donny was a year older than Kenny, who was Ed's age, and Dodi, the only girl in the group, was between Ed and me in age. Mrs. Gray was the best. She drove a manual black VW Bug with the engine in the back and a little storage area behind the back seats. Somehow, she could get all of us in the car. Since I was the youngest and perhaps smallest, although that is debatable (my mom shopped at Sears and had to buy me "husky" jeans when I was a kid), I had the fortunate opportunity to sit in the storage space. Mark, Kenny, Ed, and Brian Kennedy sat in the rear seat, and Donny and Dodi sat in the passenger seat. Amazing! Off we would go to Matheson Hammock for sailing lessons or just to go to the beach. The Grays built a skateboard ramp in their yard, and we learned to skate. When Evil Knievel became popular, we converted it into a bike ramp and broke a few bike frames jumping over it. We would make "guns" by connecting a one-foot pipe to a four-inch pipe with a ninety-degree elbow. We would drill a hole in the elbow big enough to put a firecracker in it and then jam the barrel with sea grape seeds. Kenny called me over to the house one afternoon for an ambush. He and Ed shot me in the ribs, and I went down like a wounded pig. The welt lasted at least a week and the bruise a month.

Brian Kennedy lived two houses down from us. He was Ed and Kenny's age. I don't really remember his parents; I think both his parents worked. His aunt lived in an apartment behind his house. She was disabled. She was super nice and always had Red Hots for me when I came home after school and stopped at Brian's so we could watch thirty minutes of *The Three Stooges* each afternoon. We also listened to music with her, and my favorite song then and now was the classic 1974 tune "*Cat's in the Cradle*" by Harry

Chapin. Behind Brian's house was the Bet Shira Synagogue and School. Before they built the school, there was a two-acre track of vacant land spanning from Brian's house to ours. This became our dirt track for bikes, our wilderness for spear fights (spears made from the bamboo stalks in the field) and then our BB gun fights. Not wise to have BB gun fights! Rules were that you only used one pump and only shot below the waste. Not sure who did not follow the rules, but I remember Ed getting shot just below the left eye once. That was a near miss. We played a lot of football in Brian's front yard/street. It was tough, because at least once a game, someone (usually me) was pushed down on the asphalt. I attribute most of my toughness as a teenager to how I was "taught" by my older brother and the older neighborhood kids.

Because we had a large backyard, my dad bought us an old Chevrolet junker that became our fort. We would build a bonfire, smoke cigarettes we either borrowed from our parents or bought at Al's Newsstand and sleep overnight in the car. We were quite mischievous. During Christmas, we would steal Christmas lights from neighbors' houses to "keep our hands warm." We got caught doing this once, and when we were kids, the usual punishment for bad behavior was a whipping with a leather belt. Sometimes, Mom would administer the whipping, but if we did something really bad, she would wait, and Dad would whip us when he got home. His whippings stung a lot more than Mom's. We made stink bombs (motor oil and crushed chlorine tablets) and placed them on front doorsteps. We lit plastic airplane models on fire and placed them on busy 77th Avenue. We threw oranges and shot bottle rockets over the vacant lot next to Mark's house onto 77th Avenue.

One summer Friday night Ed and I were hanging out at Mark's house while my parents had a dinner party. We decided we would walk the adjacent neighborhood of Stone Haven, Mark, Ed and I were out roaming the streets when we spotted a bright blue lawn chair in a neighbor's yard. Drawn to its vibrant color, we snuck behind the stone wall and we decided Mark would jump the wall and snag it. Mark climbed the stone wall and ran towards the chair. As Mark lifted the chair, bright lights suddenly flashed on from the house. A figure emerged from the patio door, squinting against the glare. Realizing we'd been caught; Mark grabbed the chair and ran out the side yard to 74th Avenue. Ed and I, not being very smart, ran after him. and we all sprinted down the street, hearts racing. If we had stayed hidden behind the wall and simply walked in the other direction we likely would not have been found. The daughter was on the track team at Palmetto HS and since I was the youngest and the slowest, as I turned onto 122nd Street, I got nabbed. Her father arrived and began his interrogation. He began to walk me to my house. I was calling for Ed and Mark to help me, but they hung me out to dry. I had to knock on the door while my parents were having their dinner party with several other couples. My Mom then my dad arrived at the front door, and I had to tell them what we had done. I sang like a yard bird and ratted Mark and Ed out. I do not remember the punishment, surprisingly, but I am sure it involved the belt. I also remember having to return the lawn chair the next day after we got it back from wherever Mark and Ed had ditched it. The worst of it was that when I got caught, my new gas-permeable contact lenses (read "very expensive") popped out, and I lost them. I am sure I did not get replacements for quite some time.

# Chapter 2

# My Sports Family

" *Hey coach, I got a great idea," I said to Coach Wynn. We were in the Khoury League playoffs after winning our league championship at Sunniland.*

*"Why don't we put our right fielder behind home plate? The Tamiami team isn't going to be able to hit Nick if he throws strikes, and if he doesn't, it's going to go to the distant backstop and will bring a runner from first all the way around to score a gift run."*

*Coach Wynn responded, "The rules of baseball prohibit any player except for the catcher to be outside the lines of play."*

*I had a vested interest for my recommendation because it was my job as catcher to catch all of Nicks pitches, regardless of where they were thrown. Unfortunately, we lost that game, but as league champions, it was still a great year.*

### *Palmetto Elementary, Junior High, and Senior High School*

I think part of the reason we moved to the house on 122$^{nd}$ Street was because it was within walking and bike riding distance to my elementary, junior high, and high school. The one exception was sixth grade. With the beginning of integration in second or third grade, the school district changed elementary school to first through fifth grade and created sixth-grade centers. In fifth grade, I can remember two black kids getting into a fight, and one of them peeing on the other. That was something. But generally, there was not a lot of racial tension following integration.

My favorite teacher was Mrs. Keel; she gave us all a picture of herself with her horse, which I thought was really neat. She picked me to be an elf in the third-grade Christmas play. This was my second starring role in elementary school. The summer before kindergarten, I knocked out my two front teeth at my Mom's cousin's bakery in Delaware. The bakery was named the "Three Little Bakers" and they were famous for having made Tiny Tim's, of ukulele fame, wedding cake. I had a hand on a desk and one on a table and was swinging my legs back and forth. I swung back, my hands slipped, and I landed flat on my face. Fortunately, those were still my baby teeth, but I was "toofless" for a long time. While unfortunate, it did lead to my starring role in the kindergarten Christmas show, where I sang *All I Want for Christmas Is My Two Front Teeth.*" I am not sure if it was because of my knocked-out baby teeth or just Thompson's genetics, but when my adult teeth finally came in, they were severely "bucked." As a kid, I was able to put two thumbs on top of each other and slide them between my top and bottom teeth.

My fourth-grade teacher read *Old Yeller* to us at rest time, and I cried when Yeller was put down. Gina Buoniconti was in my fourth-grade class, and that was a big deal because her father was the middle linebacker for the 17–0 Super Bowl champion Miami Dolphins. She gave me a signed picture of her Dad, which was the only sports memorabilia I had as a kid. The Dolphins' undefeated season led to Nick Buoniconti being inducted into the NFL Hall of Fame. Fourth grade was also when I got glasses. Traditional black-framed, very stylish. I was quite the stud: kind of chubby, with buck teeth and glasses. The quintessential leading man look.

In fifth grade, I had my first crush. Her name was Beth Forrest, and I would pass notes to her with boxes. *Do you like me? Yes. No.* George Strait wrote a song about it in 1995. Beth said "yes" too. Beth and I also took cotillion together and remained friends through high school and college. In fifth grade, I worked hard to try and get the President's Physical Fitness Award. I succeeded at the distance run, the shuttle run, the pushups, and the sit-ups, but I could not do the pull-ups.

During the summers, we attended day camp at Sunniland Park. It was where we played football in the fall and baseball in the spring. It was famous for a rocket ship tower with a metal slide. In the summer the slide got so hot you would end up with third-degree burns if your shorts didn't protect you going down the slide. We had bowling days and got patches for bowling 75, 100, 150, etc. I think my highest was a 100-game patch. On lunch breaks, we could walk down US 1 and get burgers at Royal Castle. These burgers were similar to White Castle burgers. On our way to lunch, we walked past the Serpentarium. We could see the snakes in the window. On field trips to the Serpentarium, Bill Haast would "milk" the snakes of their venom. He had been bitten so many times that his fingers were grossly deformed. They used his blood as an anti-venom to treat snake bite victims. We also had a "Monkey Jungle" and "Parrot Jungle" near where we lived that we would go to frequently. On the way to Key Biscayne, there was the aquarium where Flipper, the porpoise that swam in the endzone at Dolphins games, lived. When the extra point was kicked into his tank at the game, he would grab it by his mouth and flip it back to the ball boys.

In the sixth grade—no longer able to walk or ride our bikes to school, we were sent on a bus very early in the morning that picked us up in Stone Haven, the neighborhood to the east of us. The bus stop was a farther walk than the elementary school because we could no longer walk through Gray's yard. My parents had to decide what to do with my brother Ed, who is two years older than me. Instead of sending him by bus to Richmond Heights, they sent him to the "country club," what we called the Montessori School on 67th Avenue. They had horses and he learned to ride in sixth grade. I don't really recall why I didn't go to Montessori, but I can assume, as I did later in high school, that I told my parents I didn't want to leave my friends. So, I went to F. C. Martin. F.C. Martin was figuratively and literally across the railroad tracks and in a predominately black neighborhood. My primary teacher was Mrs. Grady. We called her "old lady Grady." She used to make a cone hat out of newspaper to wear when we went outside for recess to avoid the sun. I must have made an impression on Mrs. Grady because years later, when she was ninety-one years old, she came into Ed's office to have her will updated. She remembered me and asked my brother about me. It was at least thirty years after I had been in sixth grade. Remarkable!

There was no air conditioning at F. C. Martin as there was in the fifth-grade six-pack of classrooms at Palmetto Elementary, so we used to bring milk jugs filled with frozen water to school every day. We also brought mangos to school and traded them with the black kids for Now and Laters candy. I don't remember any significant racial problems while in school, but I do remember our bus being "oranged" on the way to and from school. From the neighborhood of Richmond Heights would come oranges and maybe a few rocks, which hit our bus. Our bus driver was a very nice black lady; I wish I could remember her name, and she would never have allowed anything bad to happen to us.

In sixth grade, I decided that I wanted to lose weight and get fit. My mom helped me by putting me on a strict diet. My only snacks were carrot sticks and celery. I also did some running but I was not a fan. It worked, and I lost weight. I also got my contact lenses and braces. The ugly duckling was turning into somewhat of a prince. I may have my fables confused but you get the idea.

I started playing Howard Palmetto Khoury League baseball in 1971 for the Crushers, with Dr. Pollack as my first coach. My dad was an assistant coach that year and Mom was the score keeper. Two seasons later, my dad was also my coach when Dr. Pollock lead the "Cobras" to a second-place finish in the league. One of the calisthenics Dr. Pollock had us do was the "duck walk," where we would grab our ankles and walk in a crouch. I excelled at this and was eventually made a catcher, a position I loved because it allowed me to be the coach on the field and be involved in every play.

1975 was the only year I got to play baseball with my friend Bobby Shaw. Bobby was legendary and by far the best player in the league when we were younger. In Atom Ball, Bobby was the only player who could hit the ball over the fence and out into US 1. Bobby's Dad had coached him every year before that, and when we were older, I asked Mr. Shaw why he never drafted me. I learned that the way they did the draft, I was always getting picked before he could pick me because Bobby and the assistant coach's son had to go in the first two rounds. I felt pretty good when he told me I was always a late first-round or early second-round draft pick each year. In 1975, Mr. Shaw was the League commissioner, and he could not coach a team. We won the Khoury League championship at Suniland Park, and we received rain jackets with "Pirates" and "Champions" emblazoned on the back. I still have the jacket in the scrapbook my Mom made for me.

Since F. C. Martin was a sixth-grade center, I met kids from other elementary schools, some of whom I didn't go to junior high with but reconnected with again in high school. One kid, Nick Waddell, I knew from Khoury League Baseball, even though he played in the league ahead of mine when we were young. We were in class together, and my mom took us to the Dade County Youth Fair that year. We rode one of the rides that spins and twirls and I was not feeling well after we got off. Nick insisted we rode another ride and chided me into riding the swings. I warned him I was not feeling well, but peer pressure won out. Unfortunately for him, he got on the swing behind me, and after a few revolutions, I threw up. I turned my head, and though I still had some on me, Nick got the worst of it. It was my vomit, and it was in his face! Remarkably, we stayed friends, played high school baseball together, were roommates at UF for a couple of years, and became fraternity brothers at Kappa Sigma.

Here's a funny story about Nick from Khoury League Baseball. In eighth grade, Nick and I were on the same team after he moved down to his correct age group; he pitched, and I caught. We had made it to district finals at Tamiami Park and it presented a problem. Nick could throw very hard, but his control was less than ideal. If he walked a batter, that was almost an automatic run because he inevitably would throw at least three pitches against the backstop. This was not a big issue at our home field because the backstop was just 10-15 feet behind home plate. At Tamiami Park, they were 30 feet behind the plate. A passed ball meant a single became a triple after two wild pitches. I suggested to my coach that we put a player behind the umpire against the fence so they could catch the wild pitch and hold the runner from advancing. We didn't need the right fielder out in the outfield because if Nick threw strikes, he was unhittable. I never knew this but the only player who is allowed to be outside the lines in baseball was the catcher. The coach told me it was a good idea but not allowed by the rules.

Khoury League was a great experience for me. I made the All-stars most years and got to play at parks all over south Florida. I remember one time we played in Broward County, and my uncles, aunts and cousins all came to see me play. Palmetto Junior High was from seventh to ninth grade. In addition to Khoury League Baseball, I played a lot of intramural sports: flag football, softball, wrestling, and volleyball. During spring break, we had a lot of rain, and the field outside of the school was partially flooded. We went down and found a water hose and flooded the field further, and we played mud football. What a blast! Unfortunately, our mischievous side took over. We stuck the hose into the open window of the coaches' office just outside the locker room. Somehow, the coaches found out who had done it, and when we returned to school, we were given a choice: notify our parents and probably get suspended or take a paddling. I chose paddling because I figured it would be easier than the belt at home. I was wrong! Coach Dorsheimer, the wrestling coach, meted out the punishment. He used a paddle ball racket, which was a wooden paddle with holes drilled into it for less air resistance. Man, I still remember the sting of that paddling to this day—more about paddling in senior high.

We had woodworking in junior high and I made a clock. It was pretty cool that they let twelve-to-thirteen-year-olds use all those saws, lathes, and chisels. Ed almost lost a finger building a bowl in the shop. When the lathe flipped from his grip, it nearly removed his finger instead of the wood. He decided not to smooth out the area in the bowl where the accident happened as a reminder. To this day, that bowl holds our pecans at Christmas at my mom's house and still has the groove.

I did a report on Greece for social studies, and my Mom helped me make the delicious dessert baklava. I got an A, probably more for the dessert than the actual report. A's were rare for me in school. I was always a C+ to B student. I was more interested in sports than academics. It was very frustrating for my parents, especially my dad, but they did not hesitate to leverage sports for better effort in school and better behavior at home. If I did not behave, the threat of missing games was very real. After an incident when I threatened to "kill" my brother with my 3" pen knife, they had had enough. I had been sent to my room without dinner and was angry at Ed. I got my knife and as I was running down the hall towards the dining room table all "here's Johnnie" like. My dad saw me, raised up from his chair, pointed his finger at me and ordered me to **STOP**! Fortunately, I did. Searching for answers about my behavior, my parents tried Transcendental Meditation. Weird! You were given a mantra and had to meditate, repeating your mantra over and over. I can still remember my mantra, "engawd." Not a real word, but it helped some, I guess. My behavior seemed to improve.

In 1972, I started playing tackle football for the Optimist Club of Suniland. In my first year, Ed and I played on the same intramural team. In my second year, I was one of only 36 players out of 300 to make the 75 lb. traveling team. That year we played in the Junior Orange Bowl game against Coral Gables and beat them soundly 42-0. One of our cheerleaders, and my neighbor, Dodi Grey, knew how to pronounce my name correctly and would yell it during the cheer that recognized all the players, which was a great feeling. Due to my "husky" size, I played on the offensive line, primarily as an offensive guard. I enjoyed the responsibility of running plays from the sidelines on alternating plays. During my year of travel football, I faced a challenge making the weight of the seventy-five-pound class. To shed water weight, I wore a plastic bag under my pads during the week and would sit in my coach's sauna with a yellow raincoat on Friday nights. On game days, if I was overweight at the unofficial weigh-in, I had to sit in the car with my raincoat on and the car heater on to sweat off the excess weight. Not fun (or healthy), sitting in a heated car, in a raincoat, in Miami, in the summer. But the most challenging part of this process was having to strip down to my "tighty whities" at weigh-in, which was uncomfortable for a chubby kid like me. As a result, I did not continue playing football until high school, where there were no weight limits, which was fortunate in one respect but was a challenge for someone who would never reach six feet tall.

### *Palmetto Football*

Palmetto Senior High is where the Panthers call home. My friend Bob Shaw encouraged me to try out for JV football even though I hadn't played since I was ten years old. The question was what position to play. By then, I had lost all my baby fat through my efforts in sixth grade, and in ninth grade, I was only five foot seven and weighed about 145 pounds. But I had only played offensive line, so I tried out for center. It was neat playing with Bob since he was our quarterback. Like catcher, I liked the idea of center because every play started with the ball in my hand. Coach Smith was our head coach and offensive play caller, and we ran a very simplified veer offense. Our most successful play was a power, where in a five-man defensive front, I "posted" the nose guard, and one of the guards blocked down on a double-team. The tackle kicked his guy out, and the fullback led up into the hole and blocked the linebacker. Due to my height, I had a physical advantage that allowed me to effectively block the nose guard by positioning my head between his legs and driving him back. Additionally, my time as a catcher strengthened my calves and quads, making me adept at executing double-team blocks. Our JV year was not very successful in terms of wins and losses. I recall a game against Killian where they circled the field chanting, "Cougar, cougar, cougar!" It was quite intimidating, and we felt defeated before the game began. Ultimately, we were defeated 35-0.

During my junior year, I was a varsity player. The idea was for our senior all-county right guard, Mike Wagner, to transition from guard to center. Our head coach, Jessie Davis, who also served as the offensive line coach, had devised a more advanced version of the veer offense, although calling it sophisticated in 1979 might be a stretch. One day during practice, we were working on a drill called "root hog," where two players opposed each other in a down dog position with each player's helmet locked under the other player's shoulder pads. The goal was to "root" the other player out of the ring like a hog roots in the mud. Despite not being very big, I was very good at this and beat much larger players easily. I think this got me noticed by Coach Davis.

A few weeks into awful two-a-day practices, Coach asked if anyone else had played center. I was playing guard at the time. I said, "I did," and by the time the season started, Mike was starting at center, but I was playing a half. By the last five games of the season, I was starting and playing the full game at center and Mike was back at his familiar guard position. Once more, our most effective strategy was a power-running play. I posted the nose guard, and Mike or Chris Beshere, our left guard, would block down for the double team. The tackle had an easy turn-out block because the defensive end was usually shaded outside, and our fullback, Rick Phillips, also my college roommate, would lead into the hole and "blow up" the linebacker, making a nice hole for the running back to gain yards. Nicknamed "Fathead" after breaking two helmets in Optimist football, Rickie, while a running back, was part of our offensive line group because he executed his blocks so well. Mike achieved all-county recognition his senior year and later played for the Air Force Academy. Despite our efforts, our team finished the season at 5-5 and losing key players like Mike and our all-county running back Allen Lawrence did not give the coaches much confidence for our upcoming senior season.

Our third game of my senior year was against Miami Springs High School. At the time, Springs ranked third in the state in 5A, the highest classification of sports in Florida at that time. We were both undefeated but Springs was heavily favored. They had a two-way player, Lomas Brown, who played offensive tackle and nose guard. He went on to play tackle for the University of Florida and was drafted in the first round by the Detroit Lions. He played eighteen seasons and was inducted into the NFL Hall of Fame. He was six foot three and weighed well over 260 pounds in high school. That week, I developed a staph infection in my knee that required the trainer to lance it before the game. He cut it similar to the scene in Rocky – "cut me, Mick" – and when he squeezed my knee, greenish "Exorcist" pus squirted out and shot into his face. He added an extra pad for my knee because I was determined to play no matter what. I ended up playing the best game of my life.

By the end of the fourth quarter, Lomas was so tired of me sticking my helmet between his legs and him getting double-teamed that he didn't even bother getting into a four-point stance. Instead, he remained on his knees in a six-point stance as the ball was snapped. We won the game 19–6. After the game, Coach Davis was quoted in the papers saying I was "one of the toughest centers to ever play for him," even though as a senior I was only five foot nine and weighed just 155 pounds.

## Why I am Who I Am                    Joseph P. Ludovici

Our senior year wasn't without its challenges. Despite our 5-0 start, the coaches were pushing us hard in practice instead of letting us enjoy our success. Chris Beshere and I felt the need to address this issue with Coach Davis. After practice one day, we went to Coach's office to talk to him. Chris seemed to want me to take the lead, so I brought up our concerns. I explained to Coach that we were undefeated and playing well as a team, but the intense pressure from the coaches was taking a toll on us. I reminded Coach that no one thought we would be a very good team that year and that we would like to enjoy this unprecedented experience a little more. Coach understood and told us he would speak to the other coaches about it and let up some. I was shocked. Shocked, we went to talk to Coach and even more shocked that he was willing to accommodate us. I think this was part of that confidence builder I speak of later in the story.

It was an extraordinary season. During that year, we achieved victories against Southridge High School and Killian High School, our two biggest rivals. We finished with a 9-1 record and tied for the district title, with our only defeat coming against South Miami. A memorable moment was when we defeated Killian, and I celebrated by performing the "dying cougar" gesture in front of their head coach, who had famously done the "dying Palmetto bug" the previous year after their victory. The palmetto bug is a large roach commonly found in Florida, and it was not a flattering portrayal of our team. We climbed to third in the state rankings but unfortunately, we lost to Killian in the first "game" of a Kansas Tiebreaker due to a controversial pass interference call in the endzone on fourth down. Killian went on to win the district by defeating South Miami in the second game of the tiebreaker. This incredible season would not have happened if not for our defense. We beat Killian 7–2; our defense deserved the shutout. At the end of the game, the offense took a safety to avoid giving Killian a short field. Coach Sam Miller was the new Defensive Coordinator that year and most importantly convinced Orson Mobley to play football his senior year. More about Orson in baseball, just know he went on to Florida State and played tight end for Bobby Bowden. He also won two Super Bowls with John Elway and the Denver Broncos. I ended up receiving the Most Outstanding Offensive Lineman Award as a senior and I was even named second team all-county. Not bad for 5'9" and 155lbs.

### *Palmetto Baseball*

Despite my surprising success in football, I loved baseball. I had a strong desire to play baseball in high school. While my parents preferred that I attend Christopher Columbus, the Catholic high school in Coral Gables, which was a thirty-minute drive away, Palmetto High School was conveniently located right behind my house. I walked through the synagogue and crossed 120th

# Why I am Who I Am                    Joseph P. Ludovici

Street to school daily, returning home for lunch each afternoon. I suspect the reason my parents wanted me to go to Columbus was for disciplinary reasons and academics, which went hand in hand with me. The only thing I liked was sports. I did not care for schoolwork, especially homework. When you got a grade in school, you got your academic grade and your conduct grade and sandwiched in between was a numeral for effort. One being high effort, and three being lack of effort. I received many C 2 C grades on my report cards in high school. I was a good reader and enjoyed history but really struggled in math. I enjoyed the notoriety of being the class clown and did not always put forth my best effort in my schoolwork. I distinctly remember expressing to my parents that I did not want to attend Columbus because I did not want to leave my friends and go to an all-boys school. Additionally, I believed I had a greater opportunity to play baseball at Palmetto.

Tenth-grade baseball was rough. Varsity and JV all tried out together. There were four tenth graders trying out for catcher, and the Varsity Head Coach, Bob Delgado, made it clear he was only going to keep two of us for JV. Mike Peyton played catcher throughout the Khoury League and was a very good catcher, probably the best in the league. However, he was left-handed, and Coach could not envision him playing catcher in high school. He also struggled with bad knees. Mike was moved to the outfield but eventually quit the team. Glen Whelpley was a tremendous athlete who also wrestled and played football. The coach decided to keep him on the varsity team and switch his position to catcher. Mike Sprintz, also known as Red, was assigned to the JV team. Despite being told that there would be two catchers for the JV team, I was cut on the final day of tryouts. Glen would also get some playing time as a catcher on the JV team, making him one of the "two" catchers on JV. I was devastated by the news. The JV team's head coach was going to be Bill Shaw, my best friend Bobby's dad. Bobby was a talented shortstop who made the varsity team as a sophomore. He had also been the quarterback for the JV football team earlier that year. He was the one who convinced me to try out for football. Nick Waddell, my buddy from sixth grade, the one whose face I had puked on, and Orson Mobley also made varsity that year.

I was disappointed to be left playing for the Zeros, a team of non-high school players at Chapman Park, the same location as we had played Khoury League in eighth grade. The name Zeros seemed fitting as I felt like a zero after being cut. However, about a week later, Glen decided to quit baseball rather than switch to catcher, and I was asked to join the JV team. While Mr. Shaw didn't determine the roster, he did control playing time on JV. Red was a stronger hitter, but I excelled as a receiver and had better field command. Consequently, I ended up playing more than Red on JV, although this didn't have much impact on our junior year when we transitioned to varsity.

Fortunately (that is not a typo), I injured my knee in football that year, and I was very limited in what I was able to do at catcher. Coach Delgado gained a new level of respect for me due to the toughness I displayed during the football season. As a result, Red was moved to JV while I contentedly remained on the varsity bench throughout the year, as we had two exceptional senior catchers. I use the term "contently" because, following the example of the University of Miami, which boasted a dominant baseball team and very pretty batgirls at the time, Coach Delgado had varsity batgirls who, like those at UM, were mostly seniors and very attractive. Playing my role as the class clown, I spent much of my time on the bench "educating" the girls about baseball. Allegra Hendricks was one of my senior "students" on the bench. She went on to be Miss Rhode Island in college. My other role was "chirping" at the other team. I excelled at this. I only remember playing in one game. It was late in the season, in a non-district game, against Homestead, which was a new high school that year. They were terrible and had not won a game. I was in the game late and a runner stole third. In an effort to throw him out, I threw the ball into left field, and he scored easily, and they went on to win their first game. Back to the bench I went.

Entering our senior season, Coach Delgado told Red and me that he was only going to keep one senior catcher. There were some pretty good juniors and sophomores coming in that year so making the roster was going to be tough. Red and I battled it out and I guess we made the decision a tough one for Coach. One of the battles involved "dirt balls." A catcher must be able to block a ball the pitcher throws in the dirt. Coach decided we needed to be the best at this and, set up the pitching machine about halfway between the mound and the plate and proceeded to feed "dirt balls" at us. Neither of us relented, and Coach ended up keeping us both. Red started the season, but early on, he fouled a ball off his left shin. It was nasty, and he could not play for several weeks. I took over and played pretty well. Like Wally Pipp, who lost his job to Lou Gehrig, the original "Iron Man" of baseball who played 2,130 straight games once he took over for Pipp, when Mike got better, I remained the starter for the remainder of the season. Mike did play a lot for offensive reasons.

During the regular season, we finally beat Southridge at home, which our teams had always struggled to do. We won nineteen regular season games, and we were seeded fourth for the district playoffs. Southridge was the top seed, so we had to face them on their home turf in the first round of the playoff. I was the starting catcher and played the entire game. Orson Mobley came in to finish the game and struck out the last batter. After the win, he unexpectedly jumped into my arms, which was amusing since he was six foot five and I was only five-nine. The newspaper caught the moment and published the picture the next day. It was a great win; we had beaten Southridge twice in one season (and we became the first Palmetto team to win twenty games), and advanced to the district finals against Southwest under the bright lights of UM's Mark Light Stadium. Unfortunately, the dream stopped there. We struggled from the start with the wet Astroturf, and Southwest beat us easily to end our season. Still, the Southridge victories were some of the sweetest I have ever known. I was in full throat each of those games and chirping like never before, much to Coach Delgado's displeasure. Coach Delgado was known for his strict discipline, but our senior year saw a positive change when Gene Richey, a former University of Georgia pitcher, joined the coaching staff. Richey's youth and relaxed approach allowed the team to thrive, leading to a successful season. My senior year was truly magical in terms of sports achievements in both football and baseball. While the juniors were talented, it was the leadership of senior players like Bobby, Nick, Orson, Red, Henry, Doug, and me that made the difference as seniors.

I got to play two more seasons of baseball after high school on the American Legion Post team from Cutler Ridge. It was especially great because I got to play with some of the great players from Southridge. The players who lived east of the highway played for Cutler Ridge, and those who lived west of the highway played for Perrine Post. Many of those players went on to play Division 1 college baseball. Trent Intorcia pitched for Mississippi State on a team led by Rafael Palmeiro and Will Clark, both of whom became MLB Hall of Famers. Freddie Gonzales went on to be the manager of the Atlanta Braves and Miami Marlins. Orson played for Perrine before heading to Florida State to play for both Mike Martin (baseball) and Bobby Bowden (football), two icons of college athletics. Bobby played at USF and Nick played one season at Georgia Southern.

I participated in my final baseball season following my freshman year of college, as I was still eligible for Legion ball due to the August 30th age cut-off. Returning from college with a beard, I was considered the elder statesman of the team. During a tournament in Immokalee, Florida, I experienced the hottest game of my life, catching seven innings in ninety-degree heat and 95 percent humidity. This came after a night of teaching the high school boys how to play quarters (a beer drinking game), which clearly took its toll on me. That was self-inflicted; the other time I almost died was when we were playing Hialeah at their field and one of the fans, a nice older Cuban lady, offered to give me a shave with a butcher knife she pulled from her purse as I stood on third base getting ready to score. At least that's what I think she said in

Spanish. Again, whenever we beat good teams, I always let them know it. Not my greatest quality, maybe.

One of the more foolish decisions I made in high school was joining a "fraternity" during my junior year. Yes, we had fraternities and sororities in high school. Rick Phillips and Mike Wagner founded ATROX and encouraged me to become a member. To be initiated into the fraternity, I had to endure a paddling. This was not just a light swat on the backside with a leather belt; it involved receiving over seventy-five whacks with various implements, including wooden oars with holes drilled in them to reduce air resistance and flattened aluminum baseball bats. The paddling took place on a Friday night after a football game, and the next day, I had to seek treatment in the training room. Although the issue was unrelated to any injury during the game, my backside was not going to allow me to practice that Saturday morning. I was able to resume practice on Monday, but I was left bruised for weeks.

The only benefit of a fraternity was we did have parties with the sororities and if sports were important to me in high school, girls were a very close second. I had several girlfriends in high school that were from the sororities. Unlike most schools, we did not have a Senior Beach Week. We had a fraternity spring break, but it was only a long weekend in Ft. Lauderdale. We did have a senior party hosted by one of the sororities, and my senior year it was at the Eden Roc Hotel on Miami Beach. Ironic that I later lived on Eden Roc Circle East in a neighborhood whose streets were all named after the iconic hotels of Miami Beach. That was a great party, or at least what I remember of it was great.

I was pleased when Nick came to UF and became a pledge at Kappa Sigma, as we decided to do away with paddling as part of the initiation process. Nick, like me, had previously experienced paddling when he also joined a fraternity in high school. Upon returning home, his parents learned he had been paddled and shared the story of his uncle who had suffered permanent injuries from being paddled in college. Nick made a promise to his parents that he would never undergo paddling again. I fully supported his decision to not join Kappa Sigma if paddling was involved, even with the tradition of it only being one hit from your big brother and one hit from the oldest graduating senior, as was customary at Kappa Sigma during that time. Thankfully, following a tense chapter meeting, the fraternity decided to abolish paddling altogether. I was pleased that my argument was accepted and that we were able to eliminate this outdated tradition.

### *University of Florida*

In my senior year of high school, I only received one letter of interest to play a sport in college, Davidson College in North Carolina and it was to play football. I knew my college experience was not going to include a varsity sport, so I applied to the University of Florida (UF), Florida State University (FSU), and the University of Central Florida (UCF). During spring break of my senior year, I visited my brother in Gainesville. He was a sophomore at UF and I had an unforgettable time. We went to a concert by Wendy O. Williams and the Plasmatics. She was the original female punk rocker and wore very sexy outfits on stage. That night she wore black electrical tape in a cross across her boobs. Having only attended one or two concerts in High School, it was CRAZY! I knew that if I got into UF, that's where I'd go. Although I was initially only accepted for the summer term, I had my heart set on playing American Legion baseball in Miami that summer—sports were still more important to me than academics. Determined to attend in the fall, I retook the SAT in the summer, scored higher, and was admitted for the fall semester.

The only catch was that I'd missed the deadline to apply for a dorm room. Luckily, my brother Ed was signed up for a dorm, so when he got permission from my parents to live in an apartment, it was decided that I would take his spot in the dorm. When I arrived at Broward Hall, second floor East, I removed Ed's name from the welcome sticker on the door, replaced it with mine, and settled in. No one questioned it, and this switch-up worked so well that I lived under Ed's name my sophomore year as well. During my first semester, I made good friends on my dorm floor, although my roommate was a bit quirky. He used to sit in the window and listen to acid rock on a station out of Orlando. Across the hall, some guys had an incredible stereo system, and we often cranked up Lynyrd Skynyrd's *Free Bird,* playing air guitar until we dropped. I also spent a lot of time at Kappa Sigma, a fraternity where I'd already connected with some guys during my spring visit. Unlike my brother, who could not pledge KAPPA SIGMA until his sophomore year, I convinced my dad to let me pledge in the second semester of my freshman year despite my less-than-stellar grades my first semester.

Kappa Sigma became the core of my social life in college. I pledged alongside eleven other guys in what turned out to be a very strong class. Our group included several future leaders: Grand Treasurer, Grand Master (my high school friend, Jim Cunningham), two Grand Procurators (Dennis McLaughlin and me), a Grand Master of Ceremonies (Dave Henley), and a Grand Scribe (Benton Wood). Together, we managed to both keep up our responsibilities and enjoy ourselves thoroughly.

One memorable pledge prank involved a military-grade smoke bomb meant to serve as a diversion in the main stairwell while we snuck into the house through the back exterior stairwells to "attack" the brothers. But the prank quickly escalated when red smoke poured out of the windows and doors, drawing police cars and fire engines to the scene. The smoke filled the house, and for a week afterward, everyone was still coughing up red dye. Dinners were a time for Sorority acceptances to great socials at the house, our premiere one was Luau. We dumped a truck load of sand on the back patio, decorated it as a beach, brought in a hot tub and partied until late at night. We also had classic food fights when our "chef" Ruthie and then Curtis tried to feed us spaghetti. Fortunately, we made it through Hell Week and were initiated into the fraternity. Since my dad was also a Kappa Sigma (University of Miami), he and his friend Nat Naccarato (UF alum) were able to come up from Miami to witness my initiation.

One of the standout symbols of Kappa Sigma on campus was the Beer Truck—an old beer delivery vehicle with roll-up doors on the sides. We'd roll those doors up, pile in our "little sisters" or a sorority, and drive it all over campus. Occasionally, we'd even take the Beer Truck to Crescent Beach near St. Augustine. We'd load a keg, pack in about twenty people, and head off to the beach, partying all the way there. After spending the day in the ocean and on the sand, we'd stop at a sinkhole on the way back to rinse off the salt water. The sinkhole had a rope swing, and we'd launch ourselves into the water, splashing around to cool down. Thinking back, I'm still amazed we made those trips without any major incidents. More than once, while touring Fraternity Row the Beer Truck's brakes failed, and we had to rely on downshifting and pulling the emergency brake to bring it to a stop. It was crazy but unforgettable fun!

Kappa Sigma was also known for its softball prowess. We were a smaller fraternity (in the Orange League) but had plenty of athletes, and I played on our intramural teams for softball, flag football, volleyball, soccer, and racquetball. During my four years, we won the Orange League twice in softball, and in my junior year, we won the campus-wide Kappa Alpha Kaboom Softball Tournament. This event pitted us against fraternities from both the Orange and Blue leagues and intramural teams from across campus. We later decided to host a Kappa Sigma tournament for chapters throughout the Southeast. In its first year, eight teams joined, and although we lost in the finals to a South Alabama "alumni" team, the event was a hit. Games lasted all day Saturday, followed by a huge party that night. By Sunday's final games, everyone was a little worse for wear. The tournament continued for about fifteen years after we graduated, with our alumni team coming back each year. Except for one year when we lost early on, our team usually performed well. That year we had to play nine games over two days to reach the championship. Although we didn't win, it was an epic run, and my body ached for two weeks afterward.

Our team had a strong lineup. B-Wood led off, reliably grounding the ball to the left side and beating the throw to first. My big brother, Barry Nelson, was second with an inside-out swing that sent the ball down the right field line, getting two men on base. Next came Big Nick—my roommate and high school friend—who would either hit a home run or a line drive to the fence, bringing in two runs and leaving a man on second. Hook, our left-handed pitcher, batted fourth and usually hit a home run or a line-drive double, bringing the score to 3-0. Then came Joe Leary, our solid first baseman and a sixth-year senior, who typically lined solid hits across the field. After him, we'd bring up Ken "Buf" Cooper, named after Buford T. Pusser from *Walking Tall*. At six-foot-four, Buf was a singles hitter who benefited from the outfielders playing deep after the previous hitters.

I batted next, aiming my inside-out swing to right field. Grover followed—his real name was Grover Wexler Salzer IV, so no nickname was needed. Then we had "Farmer John," our catcher. During the Kaboom Tournament, Nick threw a seed (remember his strong arm from Khoury League) from the left-center on a fly ball to catch a runner tagging up at third. The throw skimmed off the top of John's glove and hit him square in the forehead, leaving us worried he'd been seriously hurt. Rounding out our team was Tom "Broph" Brophy, our social chairman and comic relief, known to us since hell week as "Figi Island." We all shared incredible times on the field and beyond, and the friendships and memories lasted long after college.

Parties and fraternities went hand in hand. One February, we hosted a massive Valentine's Day party, taking over Phi Delta Theta's parking lot next to our house since it was too big for our own space. We invited all the sororities and, really, everyone on campus. We had seventy-five kegs and drained every one of them that night. For ten dollars, you got a cup and all the beer you could drink. Several bands played, and the night was unforgettable. On top of it all, we raised a significant amount for the American Heart Association.

Fraternities and sororities also had unique traditions, one of which was the "lavalier." When a relationship turned serious, the guy would give his fraternity letters to his girlfriend on a small necklace. My big brother Barry lavaliered Michele, a Chi Omega. I was dating Michele's sorority sister, Stephanie. Our tradition at Kappa Sigma was to "chain" a brother to the sorority house once he lavaliered someone. When we went to chain Barry, things got a bit out of hand, and they decided to chain me to the Chi Omega house, too. Chaining involved stripping the brother to his underwear and then using a bike chain to secure him to a column or pole outside the sorority house. The only way out was for the girlfriend to tear or cut the underwear, hand over a towel, and—usually—send the guy running back to the fraternity house in nothing but his towel. Since I wasn't lavaliering anyone, this was a gross abuse of the unwritten rules, and I have a feeling B-Wood was behind it. Barry and Michele got married after we graduated and are still together today. Unfortunately, they live out west in Oregon and have lived out of state for most of the last 35 years, but we try to keep in touch.

Football was also a huge part of college life. My first game at Florida Field was against the University of Miami. It was a huge rivalry back then. I remember looking out my dorm room window and just seeing waves of fans heading toward the stadium. What a sight! My seat in the Kappa Sigma block was down near the field. They used to hand out fans (a tongue depressor stapled to a gator head) for the really hot days, which this was. I tore off the stick and threw the fan onto the field. An usher on the field saw me do it and quickly I was escorted from the stadium. I was able to sneak back in after halftime, but I missed about half of the second quarter. I was there in 1984 when the Gators beat Kentucky to win their first-ever SEC championship after fifty-three years of being in the conference. We all celebrated out in front of the fraternity house in the middle of University Drive and 13th Street. Although the title was later rescinded when UF was placed on probation the following year—thanks, Charlie Pell—nothing could take away that celebration.

In my junior year, we took two epic road trips, one to LSU and another to Auburn. The LSU trip included a Friday night on Bourbon Street, an all-day tailgate with locals offering us "gator tail" before the evening game at Death Valley. We even caught the NFL game on Sunday in the Superdome between the Saints and the Miami Dolphins. Since graduating, I've had UF season tickets, experiencing the highs of the Spurrier era with its SEC championships and the unforgettable 1996 National Championship win over FSU. Later came the Tebow years, with national championships in 2006 and 2008 and seeing one of the most inspirational players in Gator history wear the jersey. Gator football remains a big part of my life.

While I was in college, my parents made it up from Miami at least once each season with Nat, our close family friend. Nat's daughter Gina was a Kappa Sigma little sister. After every game, win or lose, we'd throw a house party with keg beer, usually Busch Light for its price. My parents and Nat would stay for the party, and my mom and dad would jitterbug to the music while Nat joined in on the dance floor. Those Saturdays were some of the best times, filled with laughter and dancing.

After two years in the dorm, my junior year saw me moving in with Nick Waddle and Rick "Fathead" Phillips. Nick and I were friends from baseball, and Rick and I knew each other from high school football. Both were transferring in after getting their AAs in Miami. We shared a place for two years; Nick joined Kappa Sigma, while Rick didn't join but was always welcome at the parties with his purple bag of Crown Royal. He enjoyed his Crown

Royal. Our senior year we moved into an apartment on 13th Street, later known as the Bicycle Club. Outside there was a drainage pond that filled up when it rained, and one time, we held a mud wrestling tournament. Wrestling Rick, a solid 220 pounds and a former high school wrestler, wasn't the wisest choice—but it was definitely memorable. Another unforgettable moment was when "Fathead" came back from a party, put a frozen pizza in the oven, and fell asleep on the couch. An hour later, smoke was pouring from the oven, the smoke alarm blared, and the fire department arrived. Rickie slept through the whole thing. It wasn't quite as dramatic as the red smoke bomb incident, but it made for a great story.

Many of my Kappa Sigma brothers and I remain close to this day, particularly a trio from Orlando: David "Chow" Henley, who started the S&H Golf Tournament, an annual event that brought together his Lyman High School buddies, B-Wood, who's my memory bank for college and Gator games; and Buf, with whom I later started a uniform and costume business with. I'm also in touch with Grover, who always reaches out. There's a group of brothers from St. Pete, including Marshall Stevens, our alumni president and the driving force behind building the new Kappa Sigma house in Gainesville. Marshall's father, Ralph, served as alumni president for years before and after my time in school. Ralph was the go-to call every time the boiler failed in January, leaving the house without hot water. The new house is a far cry from our old place on 13th, which, by the end, was a fire hazard with only two working showerheads out of twelve.

Marshall, one of our best "beer truck" drivers, and Norman LeClair were tasked with bringing our "new" beer truck back from Atlanta during my junior year after the old one finally died. Kappa Sigma also became a shared bond between my dad and me, and we went to several Grand Conclave meetings together in the 1990s. These biannual meetings were a valued fraternity tradition. I held local leadership positions as an assistant alumni advisor at UF alongside Nat Naccarato, After Ralph stepped down as our alumni advisor, and even took on a national role on the fraternity's legal commission. One of my proudest moments was working with my dad and several older members of the University of Miami's EB Chapter to bring them back to campus after a twenty-plus year absence. My friend David Persky, who later became Worthy Grand Master of the fraternity, spearheaded much of my fraternity involvement. He and I were close friends throughout both undergrad, law school, and teaching at St. Leo University.

# Chapter 3

# My Born-Into Family

*"Ed sat at the bar in a hotel while visiting Ft. Meyers. He struck up a conversation with the old man sitting next to him. Ed asked, " What are you in town for?"*

*The man answered that he was here for a 50th class reunion.*

*"Where did you graduate?" Ed Asked.*

*Ft. Myers High School.*

*Ed stated, "That's where my grandfather and grandmother went to school. Somehow the conversation turned to football and the old man reminisced about the best running back who ever played at Ft. Myers High School, Eddie Hicks.*

*Ed exclaimed, "Wow you won't believe this; THAT'S my grandfather". The old mad was shocked and his amazement didn't wane when Ed said further "that's who I'm named after."*

### *Barbara Ann Hicks Ludovici*

Mom was born at home in Ft. Myers, Florida, on January 26, 1935, to Walter Edward "Eddie" Hicks and Clarist Thompson Hicks, who were married on March 25, 1934. Eddie, born on June 23, 1914, was twenty when Mom was born, and Clarist, born on

47

March 12, 1917, was only seventeen, having left high school after ninth grade. Sadly, Eddie died from peritonitis after an appendectomy when Mom was only four months old, so I never had the chance to meet him. In his honor, my parents named my brother Edward. Eddie had been a star running back at Ft. Myers High, lettering in both 1932 and 1933 and receiving all-state consideration his senior year. My brother later met an old-timer attending his fiftieth high school reunion in Ft. Myers who spoke highly of the fastest running back in the state. When he learned that he was Ed's grandfather and namesake, he was stunned.

Mom, despite her diminutive size only 4'11" and less than 100lbs., was a natural athlete, she played basketball, softball, powder puff football, and cheered at Fort Lauderdale High School. Her nickname in high school was "Burp." I'm not sure how she got the name, but it is a derivative of Barbara. Dad never liked that nicked name and always called her "Puddin'" because she made great pudding. She's still has two close friends from high school, Beachy and Lois, whom she meets up with most every year in Indian Rocks Beach. She was also involved in several student organizations. In her junior year, her class needed a turkey for a skit, and as she lived in a rural area of Ft. Lauderdale where they kept many animals, she somehow managed to bring her own live turkey to school, which made it onto the stage and made the production very authentic. Later, she continued her love of sports by playing competitive tennis and even ski racing for the Miami Ski Club. Although she hadn't started skiing or even seen snow until she was past thirty-five, she became a strong ski competitor, winning gold medals in NASTAR.

After high school, Mom went to nursing school at Jackson Memorial Hospital in Miami. She credits her school counselor with suggesting nursing over secretarial skills which she was already proficient at from taking typing classes in high school. Upon graduating from nursing school, she worked full-time at a urology group and nights at the hospital, making $6,900 a year and saving money—a trait she credits to her frugal Scottish heritage. Dad, fresh out of law school, used to joke that he married her for the money. Their first date was a law school party at the beach, a blind date that became memorable. When Mom heard his last name, she assumed he was Jewish; Italians weren't common in her circle. Ironically though, she and two of her brothers ended up marrying Italians. Mom, impressed with Dad's dancing, spent the day with him, jitterbugging in the sand. But she had already told my Dad she had another date that evening. When Dad brought her home from the beach, he joined her roommates, who were having an impromptu party with a friend visiting from New York. He went out and bought extra beer and hung out with them while Mom went on her date.

Mom clearly liked Dad more than her other date, as they soon started dating exclusively and married on October 15, 1960, in a Catholic Church after Mom converted to Catholicism. Dotsy Moorehead, her close friend from nursing school, served as her maid of honor with Connie Johnson, another lifelong nursing friend, also in the wedding party. During family trips north, we often stopped first in Lake Placid to visit Dotsy and then again in Atlanta to visit the Johnsons.

After the wedding, Mom and Dad lived in an apartment behind my Nonni's house in Miami, where Dad had been living. Mom insisted they pay rent, but when my Nonno refused to accept it, they started a separate bank account, depositing rent each month to give to Nonni when they moved out. Mom, who was twenty-six at the time, had been working since she was fourteen and had helped raise her younger siblings. Dad, who was thirty-one, had been used to my Nonna's care: she did his laundry, cooked his meals, and cleaned his apartment. So, when he tried to direct Mom in cooking or housekeeping, it didn't go over well! They didn't stay in the apartment long because soon after they were married, Mom became pregnant with Ed, and they bought the house on 124th Street for $16,000.

Ed was born on September 20, 1961, at Jackson Memorial Hospital. He was an easy baby as long as he was well-fed. Though Mom left her hospital shifts, she continued working for the urologists, so Ed was often watched by a neighbor or my Nonni. Mom and Dad agreed that the baby would adapt to their world, with music and everyday noise going on as usual, so Ed would learn to sleep through it all.

When I arrived twenty-three months to the day later, the same philosophy applied. I was also an easy baby, and my grandmother Clarist came to live with us after about a year, so she often looked after me and Ed. By then, Dad needed more help with his law firm, so Mom left nursing to become his paralegal, runner, and bookkeeper. She managed the books for many years, coming in a few days each week once we started school; otherwise, she was fully dedicated to being a mom. She packed our lunches in small paper bags, sat with us at the small kitchen table each morning for breakfast, and always had time to talk.

One morning when I was about thirteen, after a league baseball championship celebration the night before, I felt especially rough from sneaking too much champagne. Despite my hangover, Mom made sure I was at school on time. She asked if I knew what I'd been the night before, and when I admitted "DRUNK!," she asked if I'd liked it. I honestly answered, "Not really," as I spent most of the night vomiting pizza and champagne. Though she was sympathetic, missing school was never an option. Her rule was simple: unless you were missing an arm or leg, you went to school—a rule my kids would later come to know as well.

Once Ed and I were old enough for kindergarten, Mom joined the Coral Gables Junior Women's Club, which supported a dental clinic for indigent patients. Their main fundraiser was an annual cabaret show. They hired a choreographer from New York to direct it, but the dancers were all club members or their spouses. Mom—and especially Dad—became the star of the show. Even after Mom had to resign at forty, Dad continued performing in major roles. I remember him as King Mongkut from The King and I made famous by Yul Brynner, and as King Henry VIII. They lip-synched, but the songs played around the house for weeks as they learned them. I can still sing along to "I'm Henry the Eighth, I Am". Although we couldn't attend the shows, we got to go to the dress rehearsal, staying up late on a school night—a rare treat—while Mom and Dad perfected their routines. It was quite a production!

I also remember slamming the pinky on my left hand in a steel door at preschool. When Mom didn't respond to the school's calls, they reached out to Dad. He picked me up—one of the few times he took me to the hospital. They operated on the tip of my pinky, tucking the skin under the nail, so while the nail grew back, the tip of my finger was gone. That pinky's still sensitive, so I type using just nine fingers. I was a regular at the doctor's: once, after cutting my knee on a sprinkler, Mom had to take me for stitches. On the way home, I was in the back of the station wagon, and when she braked suddenly, I flew forward, hitting my head on the metal back seat. Back to the doctor, we went for stitches above my left eye! Despite numerous stitches, losing my front teeth, roof falls, concussions, sports injuries, and various other mishaps, I've - "knock on wood" - never broken a bone. I credit all the milk I drank as a kid—I still love it today. Mom was my biggest cheerleader and often my Florence Nightingale. Her nursing skills saved me countless trips to the ER when she could bandage my cut with a "butterfly."

### *Walter Edward "Eddie" Hicks*

Walter Edward "Eddie" Hicks, Mom's father, was born in Ft. Myers, Florida, on June 23, 1914. His father, Daniel Lewis "Lee" Hicks, was born on March 7, 1877, in Madison County, Florida. He later moved his family to Ft. Myers in Lee county. Daniel's father, John Henry Hicks, was born in Madison County in 1846, making him my great-great-grandfather and establishing my fifth-generation Floridian status on this side of the family. John Henry's father, Daniel Hicks, was born on March 10, 1822, in Sampson, North Carolina, and later moved to Madison County, Florida. He married Elizabeth Sullivan on April 11, 1845, and passed away in Madison County in 1896. We recently became recognized as Florida Pioneers—Floridians whose relatives have lived in the state since before it became a state in 1845. Daniel fought with the

Confederate First Florida Regiment at the battles of Santa Rosa Island, Florida, and Shiloh, Tennessee, during the Civil War. A few years ago, I read Peter Matthiessen's trilogy novel "Shadow Country", which offers a great perspective on how the southwest coast of Florida was settled in the 1800s. Many post-Civil War families from North and South Carolina and Georgia relocated to Florida after losing much of their wealth. Shadow Country recounts the killing of Mr. Watson from three perspectives, one being that of the townspeople near Ft. Myers, Florida. I can easily imagine Daniel Lewis "Lee" Hicks, standing on that dock just before Mr. Watson was shot and killed.

My Hicks lineage traces back to the 1600s in England. Captain Robert "Robin" Hicks was born in Jacobstown, Devon, England, in 1670 and emigrated to colonial Virginia. He received a land grant of five hundred acres in Chowan County, Virginia, on November 11, 1719, and became a prominent Indian trader. His son, Colonel George Henry Hicks, was born in 1695 in Brunswick, Virginia, and died in 1761 in Craven County, South Carolina. His son, Captain James Benjamin Hicks, born in 1728 in Brunswick, served as a captain during the American Revolution and acquired considerable wealth. In his will drafted in 1789, he bequeathed his wife, Judith, a life estate in his house and plantation, along with land north of the creek. He also provided her with four slaves, six heads of cattle, two sows with piglets, and much of his household items and furniture. Upon her death or remarriage, the remainder was to go to his heirs.

In the will, his son Charles received one hundred acres connected to his existing homestead, and his son Isaac received 120 pounds, his slave Dick, and 860 acres in Mecklenburg County. Captain James granted only a life estate in half of his land on Little Creek to his son George (my ancestor), with the remainder going to his son Vines. His daughter Salley Hicks Hardaway received thirty pounds, while his son James received a specified amount of land with defined boundaries and three slaves. To Vines, he bequeathed the other half of the land near Little Creek, three slaves, three cows and calves, two steers, three sows with piglets, and a large iron pot. His daughter Nancey received four slaves, two cows and calves, five pounds in currency, and various household items. He instructed his executors, sons Charles, James, and Vines, to sell his "mountain lands" to settle any debts, with the remainder distributed equally among his heirs. It's unclear why George didn't receive an equal share like the other male heirs; perhaps he had already moved to North Carolina, or it might explain his relocation.

George married Temperance Hill Clayton, and they had a son, George Washington Hicks, born in 1797 in Franklin, North Carolina—presumably named in honor of General George Washington, our first president. George Washington Hicks later moved his family, including his son Daniel Hicks, to Madison, Florida, where Daniel's son John Henry Hicks was born in 1846. By the time they moved to Florida, it was evident that the wealth of earlier generations was gone, and John Henry and his descendants faced financial struggles. Mom only vaguely remembers meeting her grandfather Daniel, divorced from her grandmother, once when her father's youngest sister, Leila, took her to North Florida.

Eddie's mother, Nellie Ann Cox, was born on August 7, 1882, in Madison County to Franklin Pearce Cox (born in 1853 in North Carolina) and Mary Elizabeth Richardson (born April 19, 1853, in Madison County, Florida). Mary's father, David, was born in 1826 in South Carolina, and her grandfather, James Richardson, received a federal land patent in 1831 in Jefferson County, Florida. My mom was very close with her grandmother, Nellie Ann. After divorcing Daniel "Lee" Hicks, she moved to Ft. Myers when Eddie was a young boy and later relocated to Tampa when my mom was very small. Despite Eddie's passing, my Granny Clarist ensured Mom knew her Hicks family well. From age two until fourteen, Mom spent every summer visiting her grandmother, who owned a rooming house in Tampa. She would either drive there with her grandmother or take the Trailways bus by herself, knowing that the bus driver, who was familiar with her family, would ensure her safe arrival. Nellie Ann's rooming house was conveniently located across from the bus station in Tampa. If her grandmother wasn't able to pick her up, the bus driver would walk her across the street after finishing his paperwork.

Nellie Ann was a strict disciplinarian, unafraid to whip my mom for misbehavior, and even in her later years, when she became quite infirm, she still wielded a mean switch. She used to tell my mom to go out and cut her a switch because she was bedridden. Despite the strict discipline and switching, Mom loved her grandmother very much and speaks fondly of her to this day.

Franklin's father, my great-great-grandfather Daniel Nixon Cox (1827–1910), enlisted in the Confederate Army in 1862 in Madison, Florida, during the Civil War. Daniel's father, Eli Cox (1765–1829), married the widow of W. D. Humphrey, Susan Shackelford Humphrey, less than a year before his death. Eli was quite wealthy, owning a plantation on Blue Creek in Onslow County, North Carolina. His wealth, combined with that of Susan, which included 815 acres of inherited land, resulted in a substantial estate. When Daniel came of age before the Civil War, he inherited this estate and was well off. However, all was lost after the war, and upon moving to Florida, he was listed on the census as a sustenance farmer.

Eli's father, Moses Cox (1733–1776), had a lengthy will dated April 17, 1776, spanning six pages. In it, he bequeathed his plantation in Onslow, North Carolina, granting a life estate to his beloved wife, Elizabeth, with the remainder divided among his three sons and three daughters.

### *Clarist Thompson Hicks Stiffler "Granny"*

I was fortunate to have my Granny, Clarist Thompson Hicks Stiffler, live with us from 1964 until 1968. Apparently, I was her favorite, but don't tell Ed. When I was four, she visited my Uncle Larry in Texas, and when dinner time came, I refused to eat. My parents couldn't understand why until they realized Granny had been feeding me for three years, and I didn't know how to feed myself. Upon her return, they moved her seat away from me so I could learn. To this day, I'm not a very neat eater, probably due to my lack of practice as a child. One of my fondest memories of Granny were our trips to the five-and-dime store in Suniland, where she would buy me candy. She was incredibly loving, and I miss not seeing her grow old.

Clarist was born in Fort Myers, Florida, on March 12, 1917. She was the youngest child of Oscar Hill Thompson and Mary Essie "Mollie" Adams. Mollie was a beautiful young woman, as her photograph attests. Oscar Hill, born on January 29, 1878, in Dooley County, Georgia, moved to Fort Myers, where he owned a dairy farm later run by his son, Joseph Edward Thompson. My mom fondly recalls the dairy farm from her childhood. Oscar Hill's father, George Augusta, born in 1837 in Dooley County, fought in the 8th Regiment, Georgia Cavalry, during the Civil War. He was wounded, as his wife Polly Ann Maranza Lewis received a widow's pension after the war. George's father, Portlock (or Porteloch) Thompson, was born in 1774, while his father, Daniel Thompson, born in 1733, fought in the Revolutionary War and received a land grant of 274 acres in Davidson County, North Carolina, for his service.

Daniel's father, John Theophilus Thompson, immigrated to Virginia from England with his father, Mathew, in 1732. John Theophilus was a sea captain killed by pirates near Barbados in 1757. Mathew Edward Thompson, a Scotch-Irish, was born in 1692 in Tyrone, Donegal County, Ireland. Scotch-Irish is a term that was used to identify Scotsmen displaced by the English and forcefully relocated to northern Ireland in the early 1600's. Our Scotch-Irish tartan is known as Sutherland "Southland" a name given to the northern part of Scotland by the Norsemen of Scandinavia to the north.

Granny's mother, Mary Essie "Mollie" Adams, was born in North Florida near Live Oak in 1886. Her father, Daniel Adams, born in Alabama in 1855, married Anna McClamma in 1881 in North Florida, where Mary was born, thus making me a fourth-generation Floridan on my maternal grandmother's side of the family. In the 1900 Census, Daniel and Anna were listed in Madison, Florida, with their six children. Daniel's occupation was marked as "farmer." Unfortunately, the ancestry of Daniel and Anna remains unknown, except that Daniel's parents were born in Georgia.

Granny was the youngest of six children: three boys—Joseph, Milton, and George—and three girls—Mary, Estelle, and Clarist. Uncle Milton worked on the first road connecting Fort Myers to Miami, later known as the Tamiami Trail. I remember meeting him as a child, listening to his stories about the challenges they faced while cutting a road through the Everglades. Thick with alligators and sawgrass, it was a momentous task.

In the 1970s, Mom's Uncle George Thompson initiated a family reunion for the Thompson clan in Fort Myers. The reunion was held at various locations over the years, but my most memorable one took place at the old schoolhouse in Buckingham, just east of Fort Myers, where the family had lived and attended school. Buckingham had a one-room schoolhouse originally constructed in 1898 that still exists today as the Buckingham Community Center. I recall this reunion vividly because there was a ball field next to the schoolhouse, and I got to play baseball. That year, Aunt Pat's husband, Clem, had slaughtered a pig, and we enjoyed fresh pork on the barbecue.

Uncle George had been a cook in the Navy and owned a restaurant in Rome, Georgia (not Italy). When my mom was sixteen, she went to Georgia to stay with Uncle George and Aunt

Fern. Aunt Fern taught her how to waitress and she made good money in tips over the summer. As a child, my Mom taught me how to set the table, and that was usually my job before dinner. The fork – four letters - went on the left – also four letters. The knife is protected by the spoon, so no one gets hurt – five letters each - went on the right – also five letters. If you hold up your left hand and circle the pointer finger and thumb, it makes a small "b," which is the side of the dish where the bread plate goes, and if you also circle those fingers on your right hand, it makes a small "d" where the drink goes. I taught my kids this and many other people, including my cousin Donna's husband Joe, who has taught his children and, most importantly, his grandchildren.

Uncle George was the family historian, and when he passed away, my mom took over the planning of the reunion and the responsibility of collecting family information, which has been a crucial foundation for this book. In the early 1990s, Mom suggested moving the reunion to Fort Myers Beach, hoping the beach would encourage more families to attend the reunion. Every June, The Best Western has served as our home for nearly 30 years. My kids always enjoyed playing with their cousins on the swing set and in the swimming pool. Each Friday night, while Generation Two (my generation) went to dinner together, Generation One, led by my mom, would take Generation Three to the Dairy Queen for ice cream—a highlight of the reunion for them. Unfortunately, the Best Western and most of the island was destroyed in 2022 when Hurricane Ian made landfall just north of the area, resulting in a massive storm surge. Despite this setback, the reunion continues, and we hope to return to the beach soon with the fourth generation.

### *Floyd Robert Stiffler "Grand Pop Floyd"*

After Eddie's death in May 1935, Clarist remarried Floyd Robert Stiffler on June 4, 1936, in Hendry County, Florida. "Grandpop" Floyd was a mechanic from Columbus, Ohio. One of my mom's earliest memories is of living in an apartment above the garage where Floyd worked. After they put her to bed and thought she was asleep, they would go across the street for drinks and dinner at Buck's. My mom would stand in her crib by the window, calling for her mom and "Daddy" to come home from Buck's and bring her a hamburger and French fries. Another cherished memory from Fort Myers was of her Daddy racing midget cars on dirt tracks. She would go to the track with her mom and cheer for her Daddy's victories. I have some of his screws, nuts, bolts, and other items from his parts cabinet, which Uncle Carl gave me when he passed away. Mom's relationship with her Daddy Floyd was a good one; even though she was never formally adopted by him, she always called him "Daddy" and loved him dearly. I fondly remember Grandpop Floyd joining us for Christmas dinners at Uncle Carl's or Uncle Lewis' houses.

When my mom was three, her sister Mary Jo was born in Fort Myers. A few years later, her first brother, Lewis, also arrived in Fort Myers. Mary Jo was born in the hospital, but Lewis was born at home. Mom was about six when Lewis was born and recalls the anxiety of trying to see her mother during the birth, worried because Granny was screaming and she thought someone was hurting her. Mom wanted to comfort her. After Lewis was born, the family moved to Fort Lauderdale, where Mom's two youngest brothers, Carl and Larry, were born at Broward General Hospital.

Clarist and Floyd had a rocky marriage. Perhaps because Floyd was so handsome, he was also somewhat of a ladies' man. They separated several times throughout their marriage, remaining in love with each other even after their divorce. During their first separation in January 1945, Granny took the kids to Savannah Beach, Georgia, to live near her eldest sister, Mary who everyone called Peg. Floyd soon followed and convinced Clarist to return to Fort Lauderdale. Mom stayed in Georgia for the remainder of the fourth-grade year and returned to Fort Lauderdale that summer. During the second significant separation, Granny moved back to Fort Myers with Mom and Mary Jo, while the boys stayed in Fort Lauderdale with Floyd. This separation was very difficult for Granny, and she vowed never to let the children be separated again. Eventually, she managed to reunite them in Fort Myers, where they lived with various aunts and uncles, at least keeping the family in the same city.

Floyd and Clarist reconciled once more and moved back to Fort Lauderdale, where Mom finished the eighth grade and began high school. However, during her high school years, Mom's parents separated for the last time, they ultimately divorced in 1968, allowing Granny to remarry. She married Earl Penny, a shrimper from Fort Myers. I remember the wedding as my dad officiated it at our home on 122nd Street. Unfortunately, that relationship lasted only a year after Granny returned to Fort Myers with Earl.

After her brief marriage to Earl, Granny was renting a house from Mrs. Schooley in Fort Myers. Ed and I visited her during the summer of 1970. Mrs. Schooley had a rotary push lawn mower that we used to mow the grass. We also bought sparklers and stuck them through the huge grasshoppers that lived in Fort Myers before lighting them—thankfully, we didn't grow up to be mass murderers!

To make ends meet, Granny had boarders living in her home. One of them was an amputee who used a wheelchair after losing one leg. I'm not sure who took care of whom, but it was a good situation for Granny, and the woman was kind enough that she never freaked me out. One afternoon, the lady came out of

Granny's room and called for an ambulance. She had found Granny unresponsive and couldn't wake her from her afternoon nap. My brother and I waited by the front door for the paramedics to arrive. I don't believe Granny was alive then; I think she passed away in her sleep. I hope so, anyway. Uncle George called my mom, who left Miami immediately and arrived that evening to ensure Ed and I were okay. I don't remember the funeral, but I know I missed her a lot.

### *Mom's Brothers and Sister*

Despite Granny's marriage to Floyd ending in divorce and my mom having a different father, her relationship with her siblings is probably the strongest among any siblings in the world. Mom will punch you in the nose if you refer to her siblings as "half" anything. As kids, we were closest to Uncle Lewis and Uncle Carl, who lived in Fort Lauderdale. Uncle Larry, a career Air Force man, primarily lived in Texas while we were growing up, where he has settled after retiring. Despite the distance, Uncle Larry and Mom remain very close; he affectionately calls her "sister" instead of Barbara.

Aunt Mary Jo moved to North Carolina after marrying Uncle Pete Loyzelle. Although we received Christmas presents from her, we didn't spend much time together. I understand that Mom and her brothers were upset when Aunt Mary Jo didn't attend Granny's funeral in 1970. She had just given birth to Patrick, her third child, and after a difficult pregnancy and delivery she was advised not to travel for the funeral. Fortunately, over the years, we have gotten to know Cousins Lynn, Catherine, and Patrick, along with their families, and we see them most years at the Thompson family reunion on Fort Myers Beach. To Catherine's credit, she played a significant role in reaching out and strengthening the bond, first with my Mom and Dad and then with the rest of the family. This reconnection has allowed Aunt Mary Jo to renew her relationships with my Mom and her brothers over the past twenty years, and they recently celebrated Mom's 89th birthday together on a cruise. Since Uncle Pete's passing a few years ago, Mom and Aunt Mary Jo have shared a room during family reunions and on the cruise. This is a valuable lesson about never giving up on family.

And here's a bit of salacious family history: Mom actually went on a date with Uncle Pete before he began dating Aunt Mary Jo!

As I mentioned, we were closest to Uncle Lew and Uncle Carl. Uncle Carl and Aunt Claudia are my godparents. I love Uncle Carl; despite the fishing trips we took with him to catch dolphins (mahi-mahi). He would always make us wake up way too early to get a head start on the fish, saying the night before that we "had a big day tomorrow" to encourage us to get to sleep. There was no Weather Channel back then, but it didn't matter we would head out regardless of the conditions. Six-foot swells were nothing to Uncle Carl; as his tiny boat slipped between the waves, my fishing trips mostly consisted of hanging my head over the gunnel, puking my guts out. Uncle Carl would say it was good chum for the fish. Oh, what fun! I can't remember catching many fish.

The three families, along with quasi-Uncle Jim (Uncle Carl's best friend) and Aunt Kathy, would spend at least two weeks in the Keys for lobster season. We regularly bagged our limit of six lobsters per person on the boat—infants included—and Dad, who didn't get in the water, would join us on nearly every trip. In good years we would go out twice a day. Most of our lobstering was done with just a mask, snorkel, and fins. We would drag behind the boat, searching for holes in the sea floor, from which the lobster's tentacles would peek out. Unfortunately, I was one of those who wore "coke bottle" glasses, so I often struggled to spot them. If a hole was found, we would drop off, and the boat would circle back.

When the uncles took a break for an Old Milwaukee Beer, after a hole was spotted they would jump in the water. The older kids and Mom were the "draggers and baggers." Once we caught a lobster, it would go into a mesh bag, and once the bag was loaded on the boat Dad would measure them. A critical job because the fine for a "short" lobster was a steep $250. Our favorite spot, "Hank's Hole," was a treasure trove of lobsters, but locating it each year was a challenge before GPS. When we found it, it was rarely disappointing. The uncles would surface with a lobster in each hand, tossing them directly into the boat with no time for bagging.

Back at the dock, the heads were wrung off, and the tentacles were used to clean out the "poop shoot." The best lobster I ever tasted was boiled that night and eaten with melted butter—simple and delicious, better than any Maine lobster. The best "bugs"— Florida crawfish!

On particularly bad lobster years, the uncles would sometimes dive the walls of the canals dug in other subdivisions, which required scuba tanks and lacked the same family spirit. There were no draggers or baggers, and usually, very few lobsters. In desperate times, my Uncles would keep what we called "Danish lobsters"— the shorts—by wringing off their heads underwater and stuffing the tails into our bathing suits. Once back on board, we'd hide them under sandwiches and Old Milwaukee in the cooler. The Marine Patrol could board our boat and check it for shorts and count the lobsters on board. I think the Statute of Limitations has expired on those charges, at least I hope so.

The last lobstering trip I took with the Uncles was in 1996, shortly after Alexis was born on July 11. While she wasn't on the boat, it was quite a sight to see Lorena using her Medela breast pump at the front of the boat before jumping in the water to drag behind it, looking for holes. There were no Old Milwaukee on that trip because we needed the cooler space for breast milk for Alexis.

Some of the most memorable trips was when my parents bought the "Cove House," named after the neighborhood "Pirates Cove" in Key Largo (Marker 98). We usually made the 45-minute drive (assuming there were no wrecks on the tiny two-lane section of US 1 leading to the keys) to Key Largo on Friday evenings after Dad got home from the office. We would stop at the Pilot House for the all-you-could-eat Friday fish fry. My earliest lobstering memories are from the "Cove House." My parents bought it in the early '70s—a rustic place with three bedrooms and only one bathroom. A single window AC unit in the back of the house kept it just cool enough. All the kids—Ed, Carla, Carrie, Tony, Danny, and I (David wasn't born yet)—slept on the floor in the hallway with the bedroom doors open, keeping us cool at night. A large great room with the kitchen, living room, and dining area didn't have AC, but we weren't allowed inside during the day anyway.

Showering was optional, and if we did, it was usually outside. We stayed cool by swimming in the canal, where we'd flip the Sunfish sailboat to play "King of the Hill" on its hull. At the canal's end lived Lucy, a high-energy Jack Russell Terrier, who would bark wildly whenever anyone fell from the Sunfish and splashed in the water. One time, we caught a grunt fish and threw it on a heavy rod line that night, hoping to reel in something big.

By morning, we had a six-foot nurse shark on the line! We spent hours working to bring it up to the dock; each taking turns on the reel until we finally landed it. That gave us a bit of pause about swimming in the canal for a few days.

The Cove House was only our first lobstering base. When getting to Key Largo became too challenging with weekend football and baseball commitments, my parents sold the house. Afterwards, we lobstered from Big Pine Key Campground, which is where I developed my strong aversion to camping. The campground itself was fun, with a game room and plenty of other kids to play with. But the mosquitoes! Millions of them. We had a travel trailer, so we had AC, but again, we weren't allowed inside until it was time for bed. Every evening, as the sun set, swarms of mosquitoes would descend. Swatting, Off! or even Aunt Claudia's secret Skin So Soft couldn't keep them away. My disdain for camping and more tales continue in my "Married-Into Family" chapter.

In addition to the Keys, we spent holidays with the uncles. Christmas was particularly special, rotating each year between our house, Uncle Lewis and Aunt Sissie's (I didn't realize until my forties that "Aunt Sissie" was actually named Elizabeth), and Uncle Carl and Aunt Claudia's. After opening presents at home, we'd head to Ft. Lauderdale—either I-95, to Uncle Carl's or the Florida Turnpike, to Uncle Lew's. Uncle Carl, a former Winn-

Dixie butcher who later worked for Florida Power and Light, always carved the turkey, though never on the table like in the movies. Uncle Lew would help, unofficially heading up "quality control" by tasting pieces of meat on the carving board.

One year, Uncle Lew's air conditioning expertise was put to the test when Mom tried a new recipe for stuffing. This one had Limburger cheese, and as Uncle Carl scooped it from the turkey, the kitchen—and then the family room—filled with the infamous odor. Uncle Lew quickly set up ventilation, but even his skills couldn't combat the powerful smell of Limburger. The next year, the uncles showed up ready for carving duties in HAZ-MAT suits and air ventilators—a story that gets told every year since and which Mom has never lived down.

Another favorite memory is our first ski trip, which all three families took to Sugar Mountain, North Carolina. Thirteen of us— four Ludovicis, Lewis and Sissie's crew of three, and Carl, Claudia, and the twins—all squeezed into a three-bedroom condo. On our last night, only a single box of Jell-O and a can of fruit cocktail remained. With her Scottish frugality, Mom somehow turned it into dessert for everyone, even leaving leftovers. To this day, if she cuts a birthday cake, you'll not only get your slice but probably a few to take home, even if we only ordered a half sheet from Publix.

In July 1976, we all packed up to celebrate the Bicentennial at Disney World, staying at the Polynesian Hotel on the monorail. While in line to head back to the hotel, we realized the long wait meant missing the fireworks. Without hesitation, Uncle Lew jumped the fence, and soon, we all followed, finding a spot on the grass to catch one of the most spectacular fireworks shows I've ever seen. Disney's fireworks are always a treat, but for the Bicentennial, they pulled out all the stops, and the little motorized speedboats were an extra highlight.

There are countless other stories like these. Growing up with my uncles and their families was truly a great experience.

### *Philip F. Ludovici "Judge"*

Dad was born on November 18, 1929, in Philadelphia, Pennsylvania, just before the Stock Market Crash that plunged the country into the Great Depression. His parents, Nonno and Nonna (Italian for "grandpa" and "grandma"), hailed from the small village of Fiugni in the commune of Cagnano Amiterno near L'Aquila, Abruzzo, Italy. Dad's early life was shaped by the hardships of the Depression, and he often said that, without government assistance, he might not have survived. Nonno and Nonna received aid—an early version of food stamps—that allowed them to buy formula for Dad when he was a baby. This support led Dad to register as a Democrat, attributing his political leanings to the lifesaving help his family received. My brother and I like to think it also gave us plenty of fuel for family debates around the dinner table—perfect practice for law school!

Despite the struggles of the early thirties, Nonno's hard work paid off. In 1938, he bought a brand-new Packard automobile, and with a few clever modifications—which allowed one child to stand in the back seat—the family drove from Philadelphia to Miami along US 1, to visit Nonno's brother, Domenico, who had settled there after leaving Philadelphia. Dad remembers the trip vividly, including flooded wooden bridges in South Carolina and Georgia. After days of travel, he spent Christmas Day 1938 swimming in the Atlantic Ocean, a memory that left a lasting impression. To own a new car and take a family vacation to Miami just nine years after the Stock Market Crash was a testament to Nonno's resilience and determination.

Growing up in Philadelphia's predominantly Italian neighborhoods, Dad didn't learn English until he started school. His teachers mistook his language barrier for a learning disability, but he quickly picked up English and proved to be an above-average student. He attended Northeast High School, an all-boys public school where he made it through the first round of tryouts for the freshman football team. It was a significant accomplishment when over 300 boys tried out. Unfortunately, the second round was on a Saturday, and Nonno needed Dad to work.

He didn't get to complete the tryouts, and I think this frustrated Dad and may have made him resentful of my sports as a kid. His work in construction with my Nonno made him interested in drafting/design. After high school he enrolled at New Jersey State College (now Rutgers University) for drafting and architecture classes. I still remember him using his drafting board to sketch out the rough plans for many of our family's building projects.

After two years of college, and with the Korean War starting, Dad decided to leave school and enlist in the army. He had trained in a Marine unit during high school (similar to today's ROTC) and was allowed to join Officer Candidate School after testing well. But when he learned that training as an officer would mean extending his service for four more years, he decided against it. Army life wasn't a fit, confirmed by his time stationed at Fort Riley, Kansas, where he endured the coldest winter of his life. Dad was no stranger to working outdoors in Philadelphia's winters, pouring concrete with Nonno, but Kansas winters were on another level. He completed his two-year commitment and was honorably discharged, ready to return to civilian life.

Despite having no formal education, Nonno and Nonna deeply valued learning and instilled this in their children. After the army, Dad moved to Miami and enrolled at the University of Miami on the GI Bill. He fondly remembered his 1938 road trip to Miami, swimming in the Atlantic on Christmas Day, a warm contrast to both Kansas and Philadelphia winters. By then, Dad had switched from wanting to design buildings to selling them. He worked as a real estate salesperson during his undergraduate days. While at UM, Dad joined the Kappa Sigma Fraternity, as did Ed and I years later at the University of Florida. He made lifelong friends, including Earnie Kent, his fraternity "big brother." He had his share of interesting roommates—like one who tuned his motorcycle indoors on Saturday mornings, much to his neighbors' delight, I am sure.

Dad graduated from UM in 1956 with a degree in liberal arts and, due to his experience selling real estate, decided to pursue law. Back then, there was no LSAT; getting into law school meant simply walking across campus and signing up. On the first day of classes, professors warned, "Look to your right and left—only one of you will graduate." Dad made it through, graduating in 1959 despite the odds. However, job opportunities were slim. He had one offer—from a lawyer in Punta Gorda, north of Ft. Myers. He asked Mom, then his fiancée, to accompany him for the interview. According to Dad, she agreed, though Mom recalls that she didn't go knowing fully what Punta Gorda was and, more importantly, what it wasn't in the early 1960s. Dad tells the story, "As they neared the office, I slowed down but didn't stop, deciding on the spot that Punta Gorda wasn't for me, I made a U-turn and headed back to Miami". If Mom was there or when he got back home, Mom likely held back an "I told you so."

Back in Miami, Dad opened his own firm in Perrine, where US 1 split north of Cutler Ridge. A red-headed Italian with a unique last name, he was an unusual figure in WASPy southern Dade County. His first office, on Fern Street, was among a row of offices where my brother and I would later go to the orthodontist. A "general practitioner," Dad took whatever work came in. He prepared wills and probated them. He handled real estate closing and an occasional personal injury case. That first partial year, he earned $1,900—no small feat, though still shy of Mom's staggering salary of $6,900. He even became a "circuit-riding" county court magistrate for Florida City and Homestead, where he earned the nickname "Judge"—easier for most to pronounce than Ludovici.

His career included some memorable cases. One, a tragic accident, involved a mother and her children whose car ran under a tractor-trailer when it backed out into the road. The two teenage daughters in the front seat were killed instantly, while the mother, saved by the steering wheel, suffered severe brain damage. Fortunately, the small children in the back of the car were largely unhurt. Dad negotiated a settlement that provided for the children and covered the mother's care. Dad created a trust and continued to administer it for decades. Another notable case involved a Pepsi bottle with a roach inside. The "evidence" sat in storage room for years, likely contributing to both my dislike of roaches and my aversion to PEPSI.

Dad was hired by a prominent East Perrine real estate man named Clyde Hinson. Mr. Hinson's father had been a bootlegger during prohibition and had brought illicit rum from Cuba right into the pier at 168th Street in Perrine and then "ran" it to Miami for distribution. Mr. Hinson became a very close friend and mentor of Dad. Mr. Hinson always drove a White Cadillac, and he was friends with a Cadillac dealer in Georgia. Every few years, when he needed a new car, Dad and Mr. Hinson would drive to Sarasota and pick up Mr. Hinson's brother-in-law and then drive to Georgia, where they attended the Master's Golf Tournament with Mr. Hinson's Cadillac Dealer. I told all my friends that Dad was playing in the tournament; I did not know much about golf back then, but Dad and Mr. Hinson would make it back to Perrine with Mr. Hinson's new Cadillac. When I started practicing law in St. Petersburg, I met Mr. Hinson's brother-in-law on a case in Sarasota, and we had a few laughs about those trips so many years prior.

As a kid, I spent my summers working in Dad's office. Typing lessons were mandatory, but our main task was removing "ACCOs"—those pesky clips that held down papers in the file folders—so they could be reused. My dad must have had some

Scott-Irish in him too or my Mom's frugality must have rubbed off. Our other job was real estate "maintenance." Dad's experience selling real estate in undergrad and law school and with Mr. Hinson's mentorship, he began acquiring property. He bought a few residential homes on Franjo Road, which gave us a memorable introduction to cleaning up after tenants. I recall one place where the roaches were so abundant that you couldn't walk across the floor without a crunch. Maybe because of experiences like that, Dad moved from residential to commercial real estate. I think my salary was 25¢ /hour, and I was probably overpaid.

One of his earliest commercial buildings was the Philson Building, eight storefronts on US 1. Dad named this building after his name and his two sons (or maybe just my brother). My favorite tenant was the Sub King, a Perrine tradition, which made the best submarine sandwiches. We cleaned out units between tenants, scrubbed bathrooms, repainted walls, and sometimes even repainted the floors—which taught me a lesson about painting myself into corners. Dad held onto the Philson Building for over fifty years, eventually **collecting in rent each year** the amount he initially paid for it.

Dad continued investing, eventually purchasing the Barson (named after my Mom and maybe me). I and II buildings on Perrine Avenue, and in 1973, he moved his office to 730 Perrine Avenue. An Afro Hair Salon storefront was located below his file storage room upstairs in his office. Years later, someone firebombed the Hair Salon. The fire was so intense from the stored files upstairs that it melted the steel joists in the roof of the building. Uncle Dave, my dad's cousin, and a civil engineer, helped us with the rebuild. Additional steel was added to the joists, and once we tore out all the drywall and burned wooden framing, we painted over the remaining fire-stained walls several times with Kilz. Despite this effort, for years, you could still smell the smoke when you walked up the stairs in the office.

As we grew older, my brother and I became more skilled in construction for these jobs, especially with our best friend, Mark Hoven, from across the street. Dad moved from buying buildings to developing them, and we built the Mayfair Building on Richmond Drive. It had a twin-tee flat roof and concrete headers; we acted as general contractors. The next summer, we built the REX Building on US1, and Dad moved his office there after my brother graduated from law school and joined him.

The hardest part wasn't the physical work, though I still have scars from the hot tar that splashed on my legs, which gave me an appreciation of 18th-century tar-and-feathering. The worst was trying to insulate a building in South Florida. The "latest" technique they were using then was Styrofoam pellets poured into the cell blocks of the wall. These featherweight pellets flew everywhere in the summer breeze and stuck to us, thanks to the sweat. I hated it, and I'm sure that was part of Dad's plan to make sure my brother and I stayed motivated to go to college. I think it was his version of what he'd experienced working in freezing Philly winters, pouring concrete or carrying "mud" plaster up scaffolding for his father.

My aversion to the work, combined with my teenage attitude, caused friction with Dad. Unlike my brother, I was drawn to sports. My brother and Dad shared a special bond; they could talk for hours about anything. I like to think they were twin sisters who never married in a former life, so close they probably died a day apart in their nineties. For me, two sentences with Dad was a long conversation. I guess it made me the family "black sheep," a title I earned from my dad's secretary's mother at Dad's seventieth birthday party. When Ed graduated from UF, he returned home to law school at UM, working for Dad while attending night classes. That was the plan for me, too—until I found a different path. More on that to come.

### *Giuseppe "Joseph" Ludovici "Nonno"*

I was named after my Nonno, Giuseppe (born on October 6, 1895), which is "Joseph" in Italian. He was the son of Felice Ludovici (born March 1, 1859) and Florinda Paone (born August 12, 1861). The story was that Florinda was my Nonna Evalina's cousin. Nonno was one of six children: Domenica, Domenico

(Uncle Dave's father), Giuseppe, Roberto, Beatrice, and Florindo. When Florinda died just days after giving birth to Florindo on January 13, 1902, Felice remarried Catarina Santori, and they had two children: Ricardo and Ettore. Felice was born, raised, and died in Fiugni, Italy, working as a sustenance farmer. Fiugni is located in the Commune of Cagnano Amiterno, in the province of Abruzzo, Italy.

One of the most memorable experiences of my first trip to Italy in 1977 was visiting Fiugni. My Nonno had drawn a handwritten map for us on an old envelope, showing how to travel from L'Aquila to Fiugni. When we arrived, a woman at a second-floor window saw us. When my dad spoke to her in Italian, she immediately ran from the house out to the fields, shouting in italian, "gli americani sono qui, gli americani sono qui - The Americans are here, the Americans are here!" Zio Ettore and his wife, Zia Eva, came from the fields where they had been cutting hay with hand sickles. My brother and I exchanged looks, realizing we had been transported back in time. Later that day, the village's bread maker arrived to sell her bread to Zia Eva, balancing the bread stacked on her head. How she managed it, I have no idea.

Another memory from our first visit to Fiugni was breakfast. Unlike in America, where breakfast usually consists of eggs, bacon, or cereal, in Italy, breakfast typically includes coffee and bread. Zia Eva noticed that Ed and I didn't drink coffee, and the small portion of bread wasn't enough for us. Within minutes, she had prepared handmade fettuccine and served it to us for breakfast. The speed at which she made the dough, rolled it out, folded it over, and cut it into strips was astonishing. At the time, they were building their "new" house but still living in the old one. When I say, "old house," we discovered that I was at least the seventh generation to have eaten at the old wooden table, which dates back to the early 1800s. Undoubtedly, many meals of polenta had been served on that table. Polenta is a corn meal spread out on the table with a broom handle with tomato sauce poured over it and grated parmesan cheese on top. Eva still used a hand iron, heated in the fireplace to press Ettore's shirts. We noticed that the old sheep pen, which my Nonno had said had collapsed in the 1905 earthquake and was used to house rabbits when he was a child was still in the same dilapidated state seventy-plus years later. Nonno loved to tell the story of the rabbit with the broken leg. I wish I could remember all the details, but it went something like this: a rabbit had injured its leg, and while it was healing, it disappeared from the old sheep pen. Most people assumed wolves had eaten it. About two years later, my Nonno was out hunting and saw a rabbit with a distinct limp. He believed it was the same rabbit that had been injured two years prior, and he couldn't bring himself to shoot it. Whether that was true or not didn't matter to Nonno, so it didn't matter to me.

According to Nonno's father Felice's birth certificate, Felice was born on January 3, 1859, which was before Italy became a unified country. Nonno's mother, Florinda Paone, was born on August 12, 1861. Felice's headstone is broken and worn, and according to Pino, his second wife is buried somewhere nearby, but no visible stone marks her grave. Felice's birth certificate showed that his father, Ferdinando Ludovici, was born around 1829, and his mother, Mariangela Paone, was born around 1833. We couldn't find their birth certificates, so these dates are estimates based on the ages reported on Felice's birth certificate. It's interesting that multiple generations of Paone married into the Ludovici family over the years in Fiugni. Reviewing birth and marriage records in Cagnano Amiterno revealed many different branches of the Ludovici and Paone families in this small village.

Fiugni was the frontier for the Papal States in medieval Italy, with the border situated near the old cemetery of Fiugni. My Bisnonna (great-grandmother) Florinda was buried in this cemetery. Unfortunately, the cemetery is overgrown, and no headstones are visible. The town of Cabbia, only a few kilometers from Fiugni, was the border town for the Bourbon State, also known as the Kingdom of Sicily, ruled by the Spanish. Because Fiugni was a border village, it became an important commercial center and once had a population of approximately fifteen thousand residents. Sadly, only about fifteen full-time residents remain. Due to its location high in the mountains and cooler climate, it is still a popular summer destination. During my visit to Fiugni in 2023, I called my brother on my cell phone. The reception was perfect, and we both found it ironic that, in the late seventies, when we first visited, there was no phone in Zio Ettore's house and only a single party line ran to the café/bar in town. Now, decades later, we were speaking over a cellular connection thousands of miles apart.

Nonno often recounted the story of how he left home at the age of fifteen because he did not want to be a farmer. He made his way to Rome and claimed that he learned to swim in the Tiber River. This must be true, as he could swim and float, but Nonna never learned how. Nonno joined the Italian Army, which fought with the Allies in World War I against the Germans and Austrians. He was captured and held prisoner in northern Italy by the Austrians. He managed to escape and hid in a haystack piled high by a farmer. He narrowly avoided recapture and likely execution when the haystack he was hiding in miraculously did not catch fire, despite other haystacks burning as the Austrians searched the field for escaped prisoners.

After World War I, on December 3, 1920, Nonno arrived in New York City on the French liner Roussillon, which had been given to France as part of the reparations from Germany after the war. He departed from Le Havre, France, and was sponsored by his older brother Domenico. According to the ship's manifest, Nonno had fifty-three dollars in his pocket, just slightly more than the fifty dollars needed to prove to immigration officers that he would not become a ward of the state. He settled in Philadelphia where Dominico lived and several of my Nonna's brothers lived as well. Nonno must have loved and appreciated his brother greatly because, as a kid, when I stayed with my Nonni at their house on 12th Street in Miami on Saturday nights (which was often), we would visit Dominic's grave every Sunday morning after church. Nonni would come down from Miami to see me play a baseball or football game. After our chores, usually mowing the grass, they would take us to Burger King and we would return home to watch "Lawrence Welk and Archie Bunker" (known as All in the Family to everyone but my Nonni). Sundays were for church, visiting the cemetery to pay respects to Dominic, and having brunch, typically at Sambo's. On the way back down US 1 to our house, we would pass Holsum Bakery in South Miami, and Nonno would always say, "somebody a maka' da bread." My brother and I always laughed at that. When he was younger, Nonno worked in a bakery that made cookies. He refused to eat chocolate cookies because he said they would sweep the floors and put everything into the chocolate cookie batch. I never liked chocolate cookies either.

Between 1920 and 1926, Nonno worked in the United States. Although the ship's manifest in 1920 listed him as a waiter, he became a skilled plasterer. In 1925, he moved to Miami to work in construction during the Florida real estate boom. He plastered part of the Biltmore Hotel, a five-star hotel in Coral Gables, just outside Miami. Coral Gables was developed with pink sidewalks, white concrete street markers, and numerous canals reminiscent of Venice, Italy. They even brought gondolas from Venice to float in the canals. Miami always held a special place in Nonno's heart, a love he shared with my dad. After returning to Philadelphia, Nonno petitioned for naturalization on September 29, 1926, swearing his intention to become a U.S. citizen and renouncing allegiance to King Victor Emmanuel II of Italy. Interestingly, he signed the petition as "Joseph" Ludovici instead of Giuseppe, signaling his "Americanization." On November 3, 1927, Nonno's naturalization petition was approved and he was now an American Citizen. Shortly after, on November 5, 1927, he was issued a U.S. passport and set sail on the SS Olympia to Italy on November 19, 1927. Nonno returned to Fiugni and married my Nonna, Evelina Paone, on October 13, 1928.

When Nonno returned to Italy in 1928, he installed electricity in the "old" house and added a new front door, which he painted sky blue. He also installed a ball-and-claw knocker on the door. When Ettore and Eva moved into the "new" house after 1977, their grandson, Giuseppe "Pino" Di Loretto, sent my dad the knocker from the old door. It is proudly displayed at his house in Palmetto

Bay, and when my mom passes away, Ed has agreed to give it to me if he can have the old Taco press. I negotiated the better deal! .During my 2023 visit with Pino, I found that the old house was in ruins, and we could not even peek inside. Pino told me that it was finally demolished in 2024. It's sad, but I suppose that's progress. I asked Pino to send me the weathered light blue front door if it can be salvaged, but we will see if that happens.

Nonno worked as a mason and plasterer in Philadelphia. He eventually became a general contractor and took on all types of construction work. Nonni owned at least three different homes in Philadelphia, but the one I remember was 2437 West Huntington Street. We visited this home with my dad, and the very nice Black lady who lived there allowed us to walk inside and visit the basement where Nonno had dug out a wine cellar for his homemade wine. The story my aunt told about him on the occasion of what would have been his 100th birthday, whistling as he came in the door from work did not surprise me; he always had a smile on his face. He was such a gentle soul, and his bluish-grey eyes seemed to almost twinkle. He loved children, always playing with them and making them laugh. The story my dad told about missing his second football tryout also didn't surprise me. Nonno was small in stature 5'3" and barley 125 lbs., but very strong and hardworking. I remember the story about him and my Mom digging the footer for the family room at 122nd Street by hand with a pick and shovel—in solid coral rock. From what I have seen of the hardworking people in the small towns of Italy, Nonno was well equipped for such labor.

In 1954, Nonno could afford to buy a second home in Miami, and by then, he was already semi-retired, even though he was not yet sixty years old. Nonni would spend summers in Philadelphia and winters in Miami. By the time my dad graduated from law school, Nonno and Nonna had moved to Miami permanently, though they still visited my Aunt Beatrice and her family in Philadelphia. When my Mom was in the hospital awaiting my birth, my dad went to the airport to pick Nonni up upon their return from Philadelphia. When my dad arrived at the hospital, he told my Mom he had "lost" his parents. My Mom, thinking the worst—that the plane had crashed or that they had died in an automobile accident on the way to the airport—burst into tears but was relieved when my dad explained they had simply missed their flight. This is a good reminder not to use words with multiple meanings, especially in sensitive situations.

Nonno was a tinkerer and had a workshop behind his house in Miami. He was incredibly crafty, making wind mobiles out of aluminum cans, creating his own jigsaw puzzles from pictures and post cards, and fixing almost anything. Nonna was more of the disciplinarian, while Nonno loved horseplay. Nonna would get annoyed when he played around with us. Nonno taught us how to play Italian card games, with Scooba (or Scoopa) being our favorite. The "sette bella," or beautiful seven of diamonds, was the most important card in the game. We would play for hours on the floor while watching Archie Bunker. Nonno had fruit trees in his yard, and my favorite were the fig trees. To this day, I love figs. I never saw my Nonno get cross with anyone; he would sit quietly while Nonna picked lint or other unseen things from his clothes. During Wednesday-night dinners at their house, Nonno never set foot in the kitchen. He would signal Ed or me with three fingers, indicating he wanted us to pour three fingers of wine from a gallon jug of Ernest and Julio Gallo red wine into an old jelly jar

that he filled it with water.

When Nonno turned 80 in 1975, they sold their house on 12th Street and moved to 124th Street and 82nd Avenue, just down the street from us. It was nice having them closer, and we spent more time at their house, and they at ours, during this short period before Nonno passed away.

One morning, my dad received a call from Nonna saying Nonno was not doing well. Since I was on split shifts at Palmetto Junior High and did not have to go to school until the afternoon, I went with my dad to be with Nonno. The paramedics came and took him to the hospital, but he never came home. Sadly, Nonno, who had been a smoker early in life, passed away from congestive heart failure and emphysema. This deeply impacted me, especially as I visited him in the hospital the night before he died. I vividly remember how much effort it took for him to breathe. As a kid, I attributed that solely to the emphysema and have never smoked cigarettes. I now understand it likely had more to do with the congestive heart failure, but it was a lesson I learned from him without him ever needing to teach it. Nonno passed away on October 7, 1977, and he is buried in Our Lady of Mercy Cemetery in Miami-Dade County, Florida.

### *Evelina Paone(i) "Nonna"*

Benedetto Paone's house stands on the hill to the left (west). It is a large, three-story house, including the basement. The initials "BP" are still visible on the cast concrete door frame above the original, large arched entrance door. I was told that most of the Evelina Paone was born on September 15, 1896. She was the youngest of Benedetto Paone (born March 20, 1832) and Maria Clorinda Mansueti's (date of birth unknown) nine children. She was a beautiful woman with long hair that she wore in a bun on top of her head. I remember only seeing her once with her hair down, a surprising sight just before bed, even more startling than seeing Nonno without his false teeth. Even into her late seventies, her hair remained more than 50 percent jet black. I attribute my good head of hair to my Nonna.

She came from the wealthiest family in Fiugni. During my 2023 trip to Fiugni, I learned that Benedetto Paone had a large herd of over six hundred sheep, a significant sign of wealth at that time, as sheep's milk and wool was an important staple. Nonna had a beautiful dowry of hand-embroidered linens with her initials "EP" on them, which have been passed down to me and my brother. As you enter town from Cagnano Amiterno, homes in and around this area were owned by Paone families. There were at least three different Paone families living in Fiugni at the turn of the nineteenth century, and Benedetto's was the wealthiest. According to Nonna's birth certificate, Benedetto was sixty-four when she was born. His grave marker, which we found in the Cemeterio Sant' Antonio, the official cemetery of Cagnano Amiterno, indicates he died in 1906. Maria Clorinda Mansueti is said to have died in 1925, but I could not verify her birthdate or confirm the year of her death.

The construction timeline for the never-completed "new" house is unclear. The four walls with arched doorways and windows still stand, resembling the Colosseum in Rome, which is why the locals refer to it as "il colosseo." It was built further up the hill from Benedetto's house. The new house was started by Stefano Paone (born in 1880), Benedetto's oldest son, with the help of his two other sons, Adamo (born in 1888) and Filipo (born in 1891). It overlooks the village and spans at least seventy-five feet in length and fifty feet in width. According to Benedetta Di Mario (born in 1933), who grew up in Fiugni, the sons held a large party when they planned to put the roof on the house. They bought thirty-six codfish and had them brought from the coast to feed the neighbors who would help with the roof. However, during or shortly after the party, a disagreement among the brothers ensued, and the roof was never added, leaving the house incomplete. Having forgotten that I had seen her family home on past trips to Fiugni, it was inspiring to "find" the front door with the initials "BP" over it in 2023. It provided me with a renewed connection to my Nonna's side of the family.

Immigration records indicate that Adamo Paone arrived in the U.S. on October 26, 1903. He settled in Philadelphia, and a few years later, his younger brother Filipo also emigrated and moved there. Interestingly, Adamo arrived with the last name "Paone" but had changed it to "Paoni" by the time he petitioned for citizenship. This change likely contributed to some of the confusion around my grandmother's last name. In Italy, there are both Paone and Paoni family names in and around Fiugni, but Nonna's family spelled it "Paone." Her birth certificate spells it "Paone," while her marriage certificate spells it "Paoni." On her Certificate of Arrival to the U.S. in 1928, it is spelled "Paone," but Nonno used the spelling "Paoni" on their 1953 passport application. My dad picked up on this and spells it "Paoni" as well. On Nonno and Nonna's 1952 passport application, Nonno also spelled <u>his</u> mother's name "Paoni." However, Nonno's birth certificate clearly shows "Paone." Nonno was certainly in contact with Adamo and Filipo during the early 1920s while living in Philadelphia, and he would have known them as "Paoni" by that time, understanding they were Evelina's older brothers. While "Paoni" is the plural of Paone in Italian, both surnames were evidently used. Despite my search for an "official" explanation for this discrepancy, this is the most plausible reason I have for the dual spellings of the name.

I don't know if they were an item before Nonno left at fifteen,

but she must have known that he would come back for her because she was very patient, marrying at the age of thirty-two. I confirmed that Nonni were married at the Chiesa Santa Maria della Concezione in Fiugni. I found the Church marriage certificate in Cagnano Amiterno, in the possession of Father Don Vito. The records had been removed from Fiugni after the church sustained damage during the 2015 earthquake. There is no marriage record for them in the civil records of Cagnano Amiterno. Interestingly, in 1928, Stefano Paone, my Nonna's oldest brother, was the Podesta of the commune. Cagnano Amiterno is not a town or village; it is a "frazione", an organization of several (six to seven) small hamlets, including Fiugni. The commune's political offices are located in the village of San Cosimo, which I visited several times in 2023 to gather birth and marriage documents. In 1928, Stefano not only acted as my Nonna's "father figure" but, as podesta, he was responsible for receiving and approving civil wedding certificates for the entire commune.

The Ludovicis say that when Nonno returned from America and proposed to Nonna, asking Stefano (as Nonna's Father Benedetto was deceased) for her hand in marriage, Stefano refused. The story goes that tensions rose, and Nonno threw money at Stefano, asking, "Isn't this enough?" He was probably trying to prove that he could provide for her as Stefano had done after their father's death, since she was only ten years old at the time of his death. While not as dramatic as the Hatfield-McCoy feud, there was certainly enough drama for a small village.

The conflict may not have been purely financial. On the Church marriage certificate, Nonno identified himself as "Joseph Ludovici," not by his Italian name, Giuseppe. I was told that one of Stefano's objections to the marriage was that Nonno and Nonna planned to return to America after their wedding. As podesta under Benito Mussolini's fascist government, Stefano would have been the chief administrator of the community, appointed by Mussolini's minister of the interior to replace the elected mayor after the fascists came to power in 1922. I was given a historical novel by Tessi Di Pompeo titled I fascisti di Cagnano Amiterno. Thanks to Google Translate, I read that despite warnings from the exhausted town doctor, who had been treating a smallpox outbreak in the countryside, the Podesta insisted on proceeding with the planned "March to Rome" festival, which celebrated Mussolini's Fascist Party rise to power. Stefano Paone is named as the political secretary in the novel and is depicted on the dais with other distinguished guests, delivering the official speech. Fortunately, the author does not name the Podesta, who is portrayed as a villain. Considering my dad was a lifelong Democrat and Nonno was also politically aligned with the American left, it is unlikely that Nonno and Stefano saw eye to eye politically. Whether Stefano was the Podesta or simply a significant political figure, he was an influential person in the small commune of Cagnano Amiterno during the 1920s and 1930s in Abruzzo.

Stefano Paone died in 1953, and his grave is in Cemitero San Antonio near Cagnano Amiterno. His headstone was dedicated by his sister (my Nonna's sister), Gilda, her husband Ettore Marimpietri, and their children, Gioracchino, Benedetto, and Jolanda. The inscription reads, "Man of exemplary virtues, lived for the good of his own people." Whether this was an effort to rehabilitate his reputation or simply to honor him in the usual manner at death, we may never know. However, on my 2023 trip to Italy, I met Jolanda Marimpietri Rocchi and her son Sante, daughter-in-law Gabriella, and granddaughters Loreta and Emanuella. They were a humble and welcoming family, embracing me from the moment we met. Despite being ninety-eight years old (born April 11, 1925), Jolanda had a remarkable memory. I may return to Italy in two years for her hundredth-birthday party, as I promised her we would dance the tarantella at the celebration. She recalled all of Benedetto and Maria Clorinda's children: Stefano, Adamo, Filippo, Gilda (her mother), Dalinda, Tommasina, Eva, Giuseppina, and Evelina. She also clarified that Maria's middle name, and the name she was known by, was "Clorinda," not "Glorinda."

Jolanda recounted meeting Giuseppe and Evelina when they returned from America in 1953. Nonno and Nonna visited Fiugni to see Nonno's father, Felice, who was over ninety-five at the time. They visited in January, when Stefano was still alive. Jolanda recalled meeting them when they visited Nonna's sister Gilda in Barete, and I was told Stefano was living with her at the time. Any old tensions seemed long gone, as nothing of the past conflict was evident in Jolanda's smile when I met her.

An interesting story about the little church in Fiugni, Chiesa Santa Maria della Concezione where my Nonni were married. When we visited Fiugni for the first time in 1977, we went to the church and noticed pinned to the cloth sash draping the Virgin Mary was a $1 US bill with a circulation date from the late 1940s. The bill had creases that matched the unique way my Nonno folded his money—folded in half lengthwise and then in half again perpendicular to the original fold. We concluded that Nonno had pinned the dollar on the statue during his 1953 visit to Fiugni. Twenty-four years later, in 1977, my dad pinned a second dollar bill on the sash. Another 24 years later, in 2001, when Mom and Dad took both Ed's and my families to Italy, we returned to Fiugni, and both Ed and I pinned dollar bills on the Virgin's sash alongside those of my Nonno and my dad. By 2023, when I visited Fiugni again, the church was in significant disrepair due to multiple earthquakes, and the altar and statue of the Virgin Mary had been removed. Fortunately, the church is being repaired, and perhaps on my next visit, it will be open, and the statue will be returned. It may be more than 24 years, but I hope one day one of my children will pin a dollar on the sash.

Zio Amalio Paone: As I mentioned earlier, there were at least three Paone families in Fiugni, and I was told by Caterina Di Pietro, Pino's mother and Ettore's daughter, that Amalio was the brother of Nonno's mother, Florinda Paone. My Nonni and father always referred to him as "Zio" ("uncle"), but this is a loose term, like my "Uncle" Dave (who is actually my dad's first cousin), and is often used as a term of respect in Italy. While I tried to piece together the family connections, I was unable to definitively prove them. As I have often said, this is like a jigsaw puzzle, with some pieces on the floor, under the couch, or possibly even eaten by the dog. I never managed to complete the entire puzzle. I attempted to confirm the story that Amalio was the brother of my Nonno's mother but could not find evidence that Amalio had a sister named Florinda. According to his birth certificate, Amalio's father was Filipo Paone, and while I could not find Benedetto's birth certificate to identify his father, other sources suggest his last name was Gennaro. During my visit with Sante Rocchi and Jolanda, I learned that Sante had two grandmothers from Fiugni with the last name Paone. He referred to one as the "rich" one, Gilda, and the other as the "poor" one. I don't believe this connects to Amalio's family to ours, as Amalio was considered wealthy because he had lived in America.

Why is Amalio so intriguing? You might think that my story is the first written in America to mention the tiny village of Fiugni, but you would be wrong.

In 2020, I read a book called Back Roads to Freedom by Winton Sexton, a U.S. pilot during World War II who was shot down over Sicily during the Allied invasion of Italy. He was badly injured in the crash with shrapnel in his leg. He spoke highly of the treatment he received as an Italian POW on a hospital ship off southern Italy and even after his transfer north to a prison camp in Lucca. However, when the Italians disposed of Mussolini and signed a peace treaty with the Allies, the Germans took control of the POWs, and Sexton's treatment changed significantly. In 1943, while being transported to Germany by train, he and two English prisoners jumped from the train in northern Italy, just north of the

Po River, and escaped. Despite his still-healing leg injury, he spent nearly ten months and traveled over eight hundred miles on foot from northern Italy toward the front lines of the Allied advance in southern Italy near Anzio and Cassino.

During his journey, Sexton was aided by many Italians who were sympathetic to the Allied cause. One of these Italians was Amilio (sic) Paone, whom Sexton writes extensively about in his book, recounting the time he spent in and around Fiugni. There are even photographs of Amalio from Sexton's return to Fiugni after the war in 1956. One picture shows Amalio standing in the doorway of the house across from the courtyard wall of the Chiesa Santa Maria della Concezione, and another depicts Amalio, his older brother Antonio, and Antonio's wife on the balcony of the house. Antonio and his wife were living there in 1956 when Sexton returned to Italy. This house is currently for sale, and Benedetta, my ninety-year-old friend from Fiugni who lives two doors down, encouraged me to buy it so we could be neighbors. She spoke highly of Amalio, mentioning that he was handsome **and** wealthy, but I suppose since he was no longer around, she would settle for me. I had to explain to her that, unlike Amalio, I was married.

Sexton writes about how Amalio Paone had lived in San Francisco and owned a grocery store with his brother Pietro. Amalio became a U.S. citizen in 1915 and registered for the WWI draft in 1918. He married Natie Brown in Santa Clara, California, on July 17, 1923. There is no record indicating that the marriage produced any children. In the mid-1930s, Pietro required surgery and returned to Italy for it. Amalio soon followed because Pietro was not recovering well. Immigration records show that Amalio returned to the U.S. in 1937, but he must have gone back to Italy at some point afterward, although the exact timing is unknown. Pietro died in Italy in 1944. Despite being a U.S. citizen, Amalio was caught in Italy when the war broke out, and his attempts to return to America after the war were rebuffed by the U.S. State Department.

In 1946, Amalio wrote a letter to Sexton (how he obtained Sexton's address is unclear, possibly through the War Department since Sexton had been a POW) in nearly perfect English, asking for assistance in reestablishing his U.S. citizenship. Sexton, who was a clerk of the court in Harrisonville, Missouri, had authored an earlier book titled We Fought for Freedom, which recounted his wartime experiences, though limited at the time as some of the story was still classified. President Harry S. Truman, also from Missouri, had read the book, and there is a photo of him holding it as he exited a plane on the tarmac in Washington, D.C. At Amalio's request, Sexton wrote a letter to President Truman, seeking his help in allowing Amalio to return to the U.S. The president's response, however, stated that there was a rule in place by the State Department prohibiting U.S. citizens from returning if they had been out of the country for more than a year, regardless of the circumstances. Amalio was never able to return to the U.S.

Remarkably, I met Amalio in 1977 during my first visit to Italy with my parents. I recall meeting a very well-dressed elderly man sitting on a park bench in L'Aquila. He was in his nineties and nearly blind, but he spoke almost perfect English, which delighted my brother and me. I wish I had known about Sexton's book then, as I would have asked him many questions. It is unfortunate how some stories are lost to time.

Amalio (1886–1978) is buried in a family crypt marked "In Memorial of the Brothers Paone of Filipo" in Cemeterio San Antonio near Cagnano Amiterno. There are markers for Pietro (1883–1944), Antonio (1875–1964), Gennaro (1870–1921), Stefano (1877–1925), a sister named Antonina Paone Giamberdino (1917–2009), her son Pietro Di Giamberdino (1954–2008), her husband Domenico Di Giamberdino (1917–2005), and another sister, Elvira Paone Liberato (1885–1971). It is unclear whether Filipo Paone was the brother or possibly the father of Amalio and the others, as there is no burial plaque for a Filipo. According to his birth records, Amalio's father was Filipo Paoni (the name variation persists), and his mother was Angela Zarra. However, there is no sister in the crypt with the name Florinda Paone, my Nonno's mother. Earlier trips we were able to photograph her grave marker in the old cemetery in Fiugni so it may be that she was not on the crypt because she had died young and was buried elsewhere. Thus, whether Amalio was truly "Zio" to Giuseppe or Evelina remains a mystery. While in L'Aquila in 2023, I reached out to an attorney, Fernando Paone, hoping he could help solve the puzzle of Zio Amalio, but unfortunately, I never received a response. This is as far as I got in revealing the connection between Zio Amalio and my Nonni. As Paul Harvey would say, "now you know the rest of the story" but really you don't because unfortunately, I had to leave that for someone else to solve later.

Nonna arrived in New York with Nonno on November 2, 1928, on the SS Saturnia, after sailing from Naples, Italy, on October 22, 1928. The arrival documents indicate that Nonna was listed as Nonno's wife. Nonna petitioned for naturalization and became a U.S. citizen on December 3, 1943. She was a housewife, and all of their homes in Philadelphia were located in Italian neighborhoods. Making learning English unnecessary. If you ever had the chance to taste her cooking, you would understand why my dad, at thirty, was still living with his parents. She was an incredible cook. We often had dinner at their house on Wednesday evenings, but her greatest performance in the kitchen was Christmas Eve.

Italian/Americans celebrate the Feast of Seven Fishes on Christmas Eve. Nonna made only five dishes, as they used to include eel when my dad was a child. The eel was fresh—alive, fresh. One year, Nonna tried to get the eel into the pot, but it jumped out and squirmed around the kitchen. Nonna, who didn't like anyone in her kitchen, certainly didn't want anything slithering around on the floor. That was the last year they had eel, thankfully. Nonna made two types of bacala (dried cod): one in a white sauce and one in a red sauce. She also prepared smelts (fried anchovies) and, my favorite, calamari (squid) sautéed in red gravy. There is an ongoing debate in Italian-American culture about whether it is called gravy or sauce. The Italian word for gravy is sugo, which is a red sauce with meat. My Nonna always called it gravy.

At the start of the meal, calamari was served in a red gravy over linguini, and I usually ate so much that it was hard to continue with the rest of the meal. I would always have a bit more calamari when it was served with the main course, just in the gravy alongside the smelts, bacala, broccoli, and red cabbage. Dessert consisted of homemade sfrappe (fried dough with honey and powdered sugar), torrone (nougat candy), and roasted castagna (chestnuts). The Christmas Eve dinner tradition was passed down to my mom after Nonna's death, although she dropped the red bacala, leaving us with three main dishes. For the last several years, my daughter Alexis and I have prepared the Christmas Eve dinner under the watchful eye of my mom. I hope Alexis continues the tradition with her family one day.

Nonna never really learned to speak English very well, but she was my biggest fan on the baseball field. I don't know where she learned the game, but she was a passionate supporter. My friends would often ask me what she was yelling, as they could never understand her very broken English. Somehow, even though I never spoke Italian, I always knew what she was saying. It was a bit more challenging for my Mom. As I mentioned, my mom was a Florida cracker and struggled to pronounce words like "macaroni." When Nonno died in 1977, Nonna came to live with us. Unfortunately, she became very sick. I believe she had little desire to live without Nonno. Mom took care of her, but the language barrier, combined with Nonna's severe illness, made things difficult. Nonna was diagnosed with stomach cancer, which was a tough diagnosis, as it was in its advanced stages, and she was too old for surgery. Mom did her best to keep Nonna as active as possible, knowing that it might help prolong her life, but Nonna wasn't feeling well and often vomited what looked like "coffee grounds." I would help by emptying the bedpans into the toilet for my mom. They had arguments—neither one truly understanding the other—but everything Mom did was out of love. I was there when Nonna passed away on April 22, 1979. She is buried with my Nonno at Our Lady of Mercy Cemetery in Miami-Dade County, Florida. Unfortunately, being present when my grandparents died became a recurring experience for me. I was visiting my Granny in Ft. Myers when she passed, and I was with my dad when the paramedics wheeled Nonno out of their house on 82nd Avenue.

Three grandparents were gone before I graduated high school, and I witnessed each of them passing up close.

## *Dad's Sisters*

Dad was the oldest of three children. Sadly, his sister Eva died just two and a half weeks after being born on March 1, 1931. She is buried in the Nicoletti crypt in Philadelphia. His other sister, Beatrice Florence, was born on May 16, 1932. She graduated from Temple University in Philadelphia with an undergraduate degree in secondary education and later returned for a master's degree in physics. She married Robert Vincent Nicoletti on July 28, 1956. Uncle Bob had been an accomplished boxer during his time in the army and was always very fit. They had four children: Donna Lynne (born on Sept 26, 1958), Robert Joseph (born on March 19, 1960, but passed away just three months later on June 27, 1960), Lori Anne (born September 7, 1961), and Mark Robert (born May 12, 1965).

When I was a kid, my Nonni moved permanently to Miami but would always return to Philadelphia in the summer and at other times of the year to visit Aunt Bea, Uncle Bob, and the kids. We also visited several times over the years. Aunt Bea and Uncle Bob had an impressive house with an elevator, which I thought was the coolest feature. They also had a huge rear projection TV, the first I had ever seen. Their country club membership gave us a place to swim. When Donna began driving, she drove her dad's cherry-red convertible Cadillac Eldorado and driving around Philly in that car made me want to flick my chin and yell "fuhgeddaboudit" like the tough guys in the movies.

Uncle Bob came from humble beginnings but became a very successful businessman. He founded the Philadelphia Suburban Development Corporation in 1960, a real estate company that develops and manages commercial properties in the broader Philadelphia area. Donna, her husband Joe Ferrier, Lori, and Mark all worked with Uncle Bob until his passing in 2016. His grandsons now work in the family business. Donna shared a touching story at Uncle Bob's funeral: each morning, he would sit in his chair in his closet, looking out the window at the birds. That's where she found him that difficult morning, with a slight smile on his face. Knowing he passed peacefully was a great comfort.

Aunt Bea's passing, unfortunately, was not as peaceful. I remember talking to her before her heart valve surgery in 2009. I had undergone bypass surgery a few months earlier, and she was understandably concerned and asked how I was doing. I assured her that everything would be fine and that it was a tough recovery, but she would get through it. I was wrong. Complications arose during the surgery, and she never recovered. The family was heartbroken. Mark gave an incredible eulogy at her funeral, and people stood in lines that wrapped around the church to offer condolences. Dad was devastated by the loss of his little sister, as was Mom, who loved her as a sister. Aunt Bea was a beautiful person, inside and out, with a gentle soul just like her father.

Aunt Bea wrote a beautiful remembrance of Nonno on what would have been his hundredth birthday in 1995. In it, she fondly described the love Nonno and Nonna had for each other and the special moments she recalled, such as Nonna greeting him as he came home from work, whistling his favorite tune with a smile on his face. Later in the evening, she and Dad would sit at their feet, playing Scopa, just as Ed and I did so many years later, and listening as Nonno read the newspaper to Nonna, with the radio playing in the background.

After Uncle Bob's death, the cousins decided to organize an annual cousins' weekend. We traveled to New Orleans, Savannah, Nashville, Charleston, Boston, and Washington D.C., with a few weddings included as well. The location isn't as important as the time spent together, sharing stories about our parents and Nonni. We hope to travel back to Italy together soon. There are only five of us on that side of the family, and it has been wonderful to see how our children and their children have formed connections. We may need to include the kids on the trip to Italy.

### *David F. Ludovici*

The story of my dad's family would not be complete without mentioning my Uncle Dave. He wasn't technically my uncle but was my dad's first cousin, the son of Domenico Ludovici. You may recall our many Sunday visits to the cemetery to visit his grave with my Nonni. Uncle Dave married Billie Burgey on September 29, 1951, whom he met while serving in the Navy on the West Coast. She was from Oregon and, like my mother, was not of Italian descent. Mom and Aunt Billie were great friends. Uncle Dave was my father's best man at his wedding, and we spent many Easter Sundays at their house on Seville Avenue in Coral Gables, which was right across the street from the Biltmore Hotel Golf Course. This connects back to the story of my Nonno plastering the Biltmore Hotel in the mid-1920s—another full-circle moment. My first experience with the Cuban method of roasting a pig in a pit was with Uncle Dave. He would dig the pit, place the pig in it, cover it with banana leaves, and start a fire on top. After 12 hours, the pig was ready, and it was delicious.

I never met Uncle Domenico, but I recently learned that he fought for the United States in World War I and was severely disabled by mustard gas. Likely necessitating his move to Miami. His wife, Aunt Anna, and my Nonni were very close. Aunt Anna lived in Miami and later with Uncle Dave in her later years. In her home, she always kept a picture of her other son, Robert, on the

TV in the living room and by her bedside at Uncle Dave's house. Robert was an Air Corps test pilot and was killed in a training exercise off the coast of North Carolina on July 26, 1943. I had the opportunity to see his flight book a few years ago, which documents his last flight. It is now in the possession of Robert's nephew, John Lupoli, Jr.

Uncle Dave had two sisters: Florence Lupoli and Erminia Armstrong. I don't recall as much about Erminia because she lived in St. Augustine and her children were older than me, but I do remember visiting her once with Uncle Dave. He took me and some of his kids on a trip for my birthday. He was attending an engineering convention where he was being installed as the president of the Civil Engineering Society of Florida. We traveled in his large Winnebago and had a great time. Aunt Florence and Uncle Johnny Lupoli lived in Miami, so we saw them more often. What I remember most about them is that Uncle Johnny had been a professional baseball player. As a kid who was obsessed with baseball, I found this fascinating. He even played for my favorite team, the Cincinnati Reds, as a left-handed first baseman. I would bring my catcher's mitt to family get-togethers at Uncle Dave's, and Uncle Johnny would pitch to me. Even in his sixties, he could still throw a fastball that tailed sharply to my right, keeping me on my toes.

Uncle Dave and Aunt Billie had eleven children. That's not a typo: Anna (1952), Pati (1953), Tony (1954), Lorraine (1955), Joe (1957), Teresa (1958), Ceci (1959), Julia (1961), Leo (1963), Joanie (1964), and Vince (1969). Julia and Leo were the same age as Ed and me, and whenever we visited their house, we played two-on-two "touch" football in the side yard. Ed and Julia would team up against Leo and me. We had a blast, but you had to be careful—the house was on one side, and a concrete wall bordered the other. There was also a large palm tree in the yard that we had to avoid until it died, and only the stump remained, which we then used as a reference point for our plays and a natural pick for passing routes. Julia was probably the best athlete among us, but Leo and I held our own. When we were old enough to cross the street, we played football on the Biltmore golf course.

During the summers, Ed and I would take the bus from our house, transfer at the station in Miami, and get dropped off near their house, a forty-five-minute trip when we were just ten and eight years old. We would spend hours swimming at Venetian Pool, a coral rock pool in the Gables.

Tragically, Aunt Billie passed away suddenly when I was about fourteen from a blood clot following surgery, and things changed after that. But I cherish those times we spent together as kids. We visited Uncle Dave in the hospital before he died. He had emphysema, and they were removing fingers and toes due to gangrene. Uncle Dave was a heavy smoker, and that addiction was so hard to break that even when he was having things amputated, he was still sneaking into the stairwell in the hospital for a smoke.

### *Edward Philip Ludovici*

I have already shared a lot about my brother Ed in the section about us growing up on 122nd Street and his practice of law with my dad in Perrine, but I wanted to share more about his family life. After graduating from UF, Ed attended the University of Miami School of Law, just as my dad had done thirty years earlier. He met Susan Utkus at an end-of-the-year party. Sue was graduating, as she was a year ahead of him. They started dating and were married in her hometown of Pennsauken, New Jersey, on May 9, 1987. I was his best man, and Mark Hoven was his groomsman. Ed practiced law at Ludovici and Ludovici, P.A., in Perrine for more than thirty years alongside my dad. Sue joined the firm a few years after they married, handling most of the firm's litigation. Ed is passionate about boating and poker and follows most of Florida's college and professional sports teams. He recently closed the law office, and now he and Sue travel extensively throughout the United States (they aren't fans of going abroad). Although Sue was raised in New Jersey, she was born in Philadelphia, just across the river from Pennsauken. My dad found it remarkable that his two sons, both born in Miami, married women who were born in his hometown of Philadelphia. My dad, a proud Italian/American, always said he had an American son (Ed) and an Italian son (me). Ed definitely prefers American food and has the voice projection of a Thompson—which is a polite way of saying he has a very loud voice and is almost always talking.

On April 18, 1990, Ed's son Stephen was born, and two years later, on January 14, 1992, his daughter Christina arrived. Stephen was an excellent student and graduated as salutatorian of his high school class. He received a full academic scholarship to the University of Florida and, after graduating, attended law school at UF, where he graduated in the top 5 percent of his class. Stephen is now a practicing attorney in New York City, where he lives with his wife, Lauren, and their new baby girl, Filippa, "Pippa," born on November 18, 2022—my dad's birthday. She was named after him, using the feminine form of his name in Italian, Filippo.

Christina is also very accomplished, having graduated from NYU and later earning an MBA from the Darden School at the University of Virginia. She married Dogan, an immigrant from Turkey, and decided to keep Ludovici as her last name since his last name is difficult for most people to pronounce. Sorry, Dogan. Christina works with Ed, managing our family real estate holdings, and recently moved to San Francisco. I suppose I should mention her two chihuahuas, Gus and Mia, or she'll get mad at me.

The Ludovici Family - 1978
Barbara, Ed, Phil, and Joe

Top Row: Phil, Ed, JoJo, Joe
Second Row: Barbara, Sue, Stephen, Lorena
First Row: Ashlyn, Christina, Alexis
2001

122nd Street Gang
Front row: Joe, Dodi Gray, Brian Kennedy
Back Row: Donny Gray, Donny Upchurch, Kenny Gray, Donnie's Aunt, Mark Hoven, Ed

Miami Palmetto Senior High School

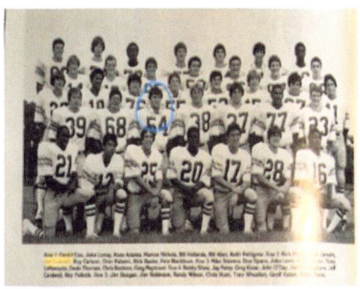

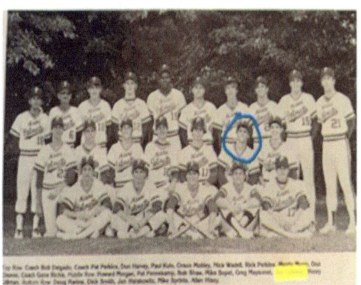

Mom 18 months          Mom Jr. High          Mom High School Graduation

Mom Powderpuff Football          Ft. Lauderdale HS Flying "Ls" Cheerleaders

Mom Nursing School

Mom Scholarship to Nursing School

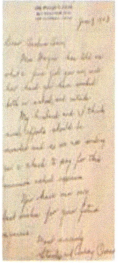
Mom Semester Paid For

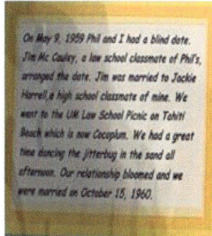

On May 9, 1959 Phil and I had a blind date. Jim Mc Cauley, a law school classmate of Phil's, arranged the date. Jim was married to Jackie Harrell, a high school classmate of mine. We went to the UM Law School Picnic on Tahiti Beach which is now Cocoplum. We had a great time dancing the jitterbug in the sand all afternoon. Our relationship bloomed and we were married on October 15, 1960.

Mom and Dad's First Date

Dad "Bippo" - Age 8

Dad's HS Graduation

Dad in a very cold Kansas - 1953

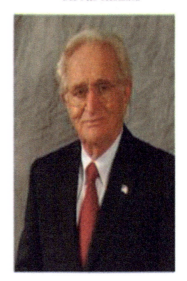

Dad in 2005

Nonno, Nonna, Dad - 1950's

Aunt Beatrice Ludovici and Dad - 1954

Dad and Uncle Dave
October 15, 1960

Joe, Dad and Ed

Dad and Nonna - 1976
Nonna was always happy when people were eating

Dad - Christmas

Barbara Ann Hicks and Philip F. Ludovici
October 15, 1960

Clarist Thompson Hicks Stiffler          Clarist (3) Milking Cow on Father's Dairy Farm

Clarist Birth Certificate

Walter Edward "Eddie" Hicks

Eddie in National Guard

Eddie and Clarist 1934

**Eddie Hicks Dies; Was Football Star**

Walter Edward Hicks, 30, died last night at Lee Memorial hospital after an illness of six weeks. Mr. Hicks, an automobile mechanic at the Orange State Truck and Tractor Co., has lived in Fort Myers for many years. He recently graduated from Fort Myers high school and was a star lineman on the Green Wave football squad.

He is survived by his wife, Mrs. Clarist Hicks and a daughter, Barbara Ann, his father and mother, Mr. and Mrs. Daniel Lee Hicks, a brother, Leon Hicks, three sisters, Mrs. Clyde Nation and Miss Lela Hicks of Fort Myers and Mrs. Elsie Kemp of Sarasota.

Funeral arrangements will be announced later by Lawrence A. Powell who is in charge.

Eddies Obituary

Daniel Lewis "Lee" Hicks          Nellie Ann Cox Hicks
Married December 18, 1898

Mary Elizabeth Richardson & Franklin Pierce Cox          Franklin Pierce Cox - Headstone
Nellie Ann's Mother and Father                Buried in Ft. Myers Cemetery

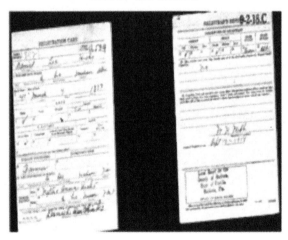

Captain James Benjamin Hicks Sr. Will - March 20, 1789
Author's 6th Great Grandfather

Daniel Lewis "Lee" Hicks WWI Draft Card

Oscar Hill Thompson and
ary Essie "Mollie" Adams with Mom 3 Mos.

Mary Essie "Mollie" Adams
Mom's Grandmother

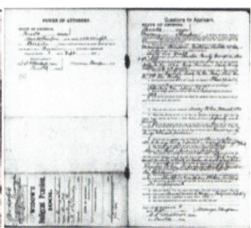

Mary Maranza "Polly Ann" Lewis
Thompson – Oscar Hill's Mom

George Augusta Thompson Civil War Pension
Oscar Hill's Father

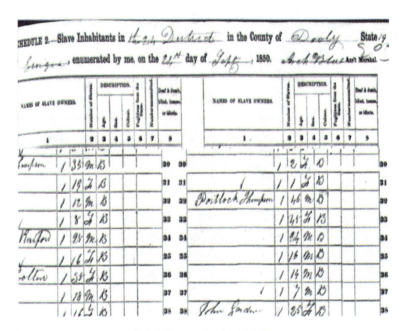

Portlock Thompson Slave Schedule 1850

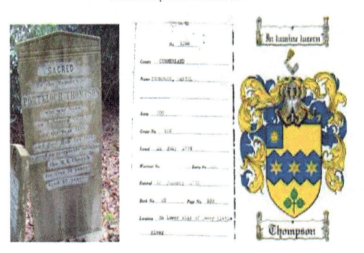

Porteloch "Portlock" Thompson
Born: 1794, Died: Oct.11, 1856

Daniel Thompson Land Grant
200 Acres - July 22, 1774

Thompson Family Crest
1732 Donegal, Ireland

Mary Jo Stiffler Lozelle

Floyd Lewis Stiffler

Barbara, Floyd. Clarist, Mary Jo
Carl, Larry, Lewis – 1946

Carl Hill Stiffler

Robert Larry Stiffler

Giuseppe "Joseph" Ludovici and Evelina Paone Ludovici

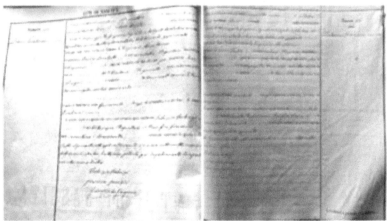

Evelina Paone Birth Certificate
September 15, 1896.

Giuseppe Ludovici Birth Certificate
October 6, 1895.

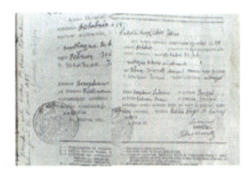

Nonno and Nonna's Marriage Certificate - October 15, 1928
With Archbishops Stamp 1932

SS Roussillon - Nonno's Ship 1920          SS Saturnia - Nonno and Nonna's Ship 1928

Manifest SS Roussillon - 1920

Saturnia Manifest - 1928

Benedetto Paone
March 20, 1832 – September 24, 1906

Benedetto Paone House - Fiugni

Zio Stefano                  The Colosseo

Sante, Emanuela, Loreta, Gabriella Rocchi
and "the Queen" Yolanda (age 99)
Barete, L'Aquila, Abruzzo

Felice Ludovici – 1953    Bisnonna Caterina & Bisnonno Felice    Felice Birth Certificate - 1859

Felice Ludovici Headstone
1859 – 1956
Cemeterio San Antonio

Florinda Paone Ludovici Headstone
1866 - 1902
Old Cemetery in Frugn

Front Door of Old Ludovici House
Fragni, Italy

Knocker from front Door
Installed by Nonno 1927

New Ludovici House
Fragni, Italy

## Zio Amalio Paone

Amalio Paone Birth Certificate
April 20, 1886

Amalio Paone Grave
Cemeterio San Antonio

Amalio Paone House
Fragni, Abruzzo, Italy

Welcome to Fiugni

Chiesa Santa Maria della Concezione in Fiugni

## My Fiugni Guides

Giuseppe "Pino" DiLoreto

Giuseppe, Marisa and Nello

Pasqualina and Benedetta

134

Nicoletti Family - 2006
Mark, Donna, Bea, Bob, Lori

David F. Ludovici Family
First row: Julia, Joanie, Ceci, Leo
Second Row: Uncle Dave, Vince, Aunt Billie, Teresa
Third Row: Anna Marie, Pati, Tony, Lorraine, Joe

Ed, Sue, Christina and Stephen - 2004

Ed, Sue Christina, Gus, Dogan, Mia, Lauren, Stephen - 2022

## MY FAMILY

Alexis - 2018
University of Florida

Ashlyn - 2022
University of Florida

JoJo - 2020
Jesuit High School

JoJo, Ashlyn, Joe, Alexis and Lorena - 2019
Venice, Italy

# Chapter 4

# My Law School Family

*We sat on the telephone pole which lay on the ground near the Publix in Pasadena eating our ice cream.*

*Me, Patten, Jay, John and Ken. Patton asks, "so where did you go after we were done studying last night". I stuttered "uhm what do you mean, I went back to my apartment on 4th street".*

*No you didn't, I waited for you at the exit to Lorena's apartment and you never came out." "I...I went out the other exit". "There is no other exit". "Damn".*

*I was busted, "yeah I went back up to Lorena's apartment, we are dating". The downed telephone pole was thereafter forever named the "Log of Truth".*

### *My Not-So-Direct Journey to Stetson College of Law*

Prior to graduating from the University of Florida in the spring of 1985, I took the LSAT (the law school admissions test). I applied to several law schools, including Stetson University College of Law in Gulfport, Florida, just south of St. Petersburg. I had a letter of recommendation from Ernie Sams, a renowned trial attorney from Miami whom my dad knew and who had graduated from Stetson. Stetson had a reputation as a great trial advocacy

138

school, and I fancied myself as a future trial attorney. I knew I didn't want to return to Perrine and be a real estate attorney and work with my dad and brother. Unfortunately, I wasn't admitted to Stetson in 1985. This left me with the option of attending the University of Miami or the South Texas School of Law, the two schools where I had been accepted.

Why the South Texas School of Law? It was the alma mater of Peter Capua, a dear friend of my father who had once been the Republican candidate for lieutenant governor in Florida. Campaigning for him had been a fun experience. I applied to South Texas and even took a trip to visit Houston. The school was located in downtown Houston in a high-rise building. Mr. Capua's son, Peter, was about to graduate, and his daughter, Andrea, was in her first year. It was a great weekend. We had all grown up together and had memorable Fourth of July celebrations with their family. Mr. Capua played the drums professionally, and had a military battle drum, which he played while the rest of us carried flags and marched up and down the street with him, keeping the cadence. It must have been quite a spectacle. A few years later Mr. Capua's other daughter, Marissa, and other son, Paul, also graduated from South Texas. Despite the positive experience, I decided it wasn't the right fit for me. Ironically, when I moved to Tampa, I discovered that almost half the lawyers in the state attorney's office in Hillsborough County had graduated from South

Texas. E. J. Salcines, the former state attorney and a current Second District Court of Appeal judge, was a contemporary of Mr. Capua and a strong advocate for South Texas, especially for Latin students from East Tampa. When I met him and told him about the connection, he recounted the story of being rejected by Stetson in the 1950s due to his Spanish heritage. When we moved to our home in Odessa, we ended up living next door to Judge Salcines' sister and her husband, the Fernandezes – another small-world connection.

My choices were narrowed down to UM or... I chose "or." When I told my dad that I wasn't going to UM, he was very disappointed. I had returned home after graduating from U; I don't think he kicked me out but living at home wasn't going to work. I needed to find a job and a new place to live. I started searching for teaching positions, but without a teaching certificate, I couldn't work in the public schools. My job search did not go well. At a point of near desperation—and reconsideration of my decision—I saw an ad in the newspaper for Gulliver Preparatory School. They needed a history teacher and an assistant football and baseball coach. It was the perfect job, and the school was only minutes from where I had grown up. I had been a History major in college and played football and baseball in high school. I met with Mr. Williams, the headmaster, and he offered me the job: $17,000 for teaching and $1,000 each for coaching football and baseball. Now, I just needed to find a cheap place to live.

Across the street from the Capua's home in South Miami was a large house with two servant-quarter houses out back. These were one bedrooms, clap-wood efficiencies with a kitchen and living room. They even had a wood-burning fireplace. More importantly, they had air conditioning. I can't remember what the rent was, but it was cheap.

The only problem was that it came with uninvited pets—pests, to be exact. RATS. Lots of them. I would be sitting on the couch watching TV at night, and a rat would dart across the mantel of the fireplace. Although I'm not particularly squeamish, having dealt with roaches as a kid, I am not a fan of rats. I set traps and baits, and the problem was, they worked. Dead rats in traps had to be disposed of, and worse, dying rats would crawl into hidden places and die, making finding them a challenge. The smell went away after about a month. At least the immediate issue was solved, and I could watch TV without interruption. The property had lots of mango trees, attracting more wildlife to my "home." One morning, I woke up to a chewing sound directly above my bed. Whatever it was, seemed determined to chew through the ceiling and drop onto my face—or so I imagined. Fortunately, that never happened, and my face remained unchewed.

Teaching and coaching went well. I had a great mentor in Mr. Stevens, my department head, who helped me with lesson plans and class outlines and provided plenty of encouragement. He was also the golf coach, and that's when I started playing golf—a game I've enjoyed ever since. Steve Hoffman was the offensive coordinator for the varsity football team and had played QB in college. After college, he earned tryouts in the NFL as a punter and later coached kickers and punters with Jimmy Johnson at UM before moving on to coach for the Cowboys when Johnson was hired. Steve ended up with two Super Bowl rings, quite the rise from 2A high school ball to the NFL in just five years. All the coaches were good to me. I served as the JV offensive coordinator, calling plays on Thursday, and on Friday, I signaled in the plays Steve called. The Thursday-night coaches' meetings were a blast, full of laughter and beer. This often led to movie days on Fridays in my class, but Mr. Stevens never said a word.

Baseball was easier to coach, involving less yelling and intensity compared to football. Our team gained some notoriety when, at one point, we had five players hitting over .500. The local paper came out to cover the story, and the head coach attributed our success to hitting practice using tees. In reality, our "tees" were traffic cones, which made for an interesting story.

The next year, I received a raise: $19,000 for teaching, plus the same $1,000 each for football and baseball coaching. When calculated by the hour, especially during football season, my pay was barely at minimum wage. Although I was having fun, I realized that long-term teaching wasn't going to provide the financial stability I wanted. So, I decided to reapply to law school. Stetson was once again my first choice, and this time I had a bit of an advantage because Dave Persky, who had been our District Grand Master for our fraternity in college, worked in the admissions office at Stetson. I reached out to him for assistance, and Dave arranged a personal interview for me with the dean of admissions. I'm not sure whether it was the interview or my teaching experience, but I was accepted to start in May 1987. Gulliver's school year wouldn't end until late May, but Mr. Stevens and Mr. Williams were very gracious and allowed me to leave early.

My dad and I hadn't spoken much over those two years, but I think he began to respect me for making my own decisions. His offer to loan me the money for law school, interest-free, was still on the table. My parents had loaned me money for my undergraduate studies at UF, but they made it clear that it was a loan, with the expectation of repayment. They required me to sign a promissory note for any money they sent. Before heading to law school, I managed to repay $10,000 from my two years of teaching. I doubt I'll ever save that high a percentage of my income again.

I packed up a U-Haul trailer and set out for St. Petersburg, where Stetson's law school is located. I had to borrow my brother's Oldsmobile because my Grand Am didn't have a trailer hitch. When I reached the Skyway Bridge, just south of St. Pete, the Oldsmobile struggled to make it up the incline. It was smoking and overheating, and for a moment, I thought I might end up rolling backward down the bridge. But I made it to law school, just barely—both figuratively and literally.

### *Stetson College of Law*

In May 1987, I moved into an apartment in North St. Pete with Bob Shaw, who had graduated from USF and was bartending at Chili's near the USF campus while waiting to secure a teaching job in Pinellas County. Bob was a Phi Delta Theta'sa Theta'sa Theta from USF and had met another Phi Delta Theta'sa Theta'sa from the University of Florida, Patton (like the general) Youngblood, who was working at Chili's as a server. Knowing that Patton was also starting at Stetson, Bob told me to make sure I found him there. I believe we met on the first day. Summer admissions at Stetson were generally reserved for non-traditional students (in my case, that meant not having been academically stellar in undergrad), and Patton fit that description as well. That short semester, we took three classes: Real Property with Dean Richard

144

Dillon, Contracts with Professor Michael Swigert, and Research and Writing I with Professor Susan Armstrong. Patton and I quickly realized that law school was going to be a significant challenge, but we were both confident—perhaps overly so.

Dean Dillon was no longer the dean of the law school, but he was known as the main reason many graduates from the 1970s never donated to Stetson. He had a reputation for being a poor dean and generally sour. For comparison, think of Professor Kingsfield, the John Houseman character from the 1973 film "The Paper Chase". Despite his intimidating presence, Patton and I weren't as fazed as other students were. In fact, we found humor in many of Dean Dillon's mannerisms. Patton was especially good at mimicking the dean's Southern drawl, particularly his go-to line, "whatcha gonna do about that," which he used when he thought he had a student cornered. This happened often during discussions about the rule against perpetuities, the rule in Shelly's case, or other complex real property concepts. More on Dean Dillon later.

Professor Swigert was unpredictable, likely due to some chemical imbalance. At times, he was kind and gentle, but without warning, he would fly off the handle and lash out at a student. He had a sort of stray eye, so you were never really sure if his anger was directed at you or the person two seats over. For reference, think of Dr. Brown from Back to the Future. By our final year, when I took Professor Swigert for a jurisprudence class, he seemed to have mellowed out or found the right medication, and I actually grew to like him. Perhaps he was playing a role during our first year, but who knows.

Our biggest struggle was in Research and Writing. I struggled because I was not a strong writer, while Patton's challenge was getting assignments turned in on time. In 1987, law school did not have the abundance of computers we see today. My parents had given me a "word processor," which was a significant step up from a typewriter but nothing like WordPerfect or Word. Patton had a typewriter, so when I finished my assignments, I would let him use my word processor. He was an excellent writer, but without fail, he would be sprinting from his dorm room at 1:59 p.m. across Stetson's courtyard to submit his paper by the 2:00 p.m. deadline, usually more like 2:03 p.m. Thankfully, Professor Armstrong was not overly strict about submission times. This habit of Patton's continued throughout law school, and if you look at our class photo on graduation day, you'll spot Patton at the end of the row, cap askew and sweating, because he had just sprinted across the courtyard that hot December day (and it's always hot in Florida), barely making it into the picture.

So why were we so confident? My confidence came from my experience standing in front of teenagers for the past two years and from my background in sports. Patton also had a sports background, though his was far more impressive. He was a junior golf champion and, despite never playing football growing up, he walked on at UF as an outside linebacker. In the early eighties, UF had a future NFL Hall of Fame linebacker named Wilber Marshall. Going up against Wilber in practice every day made Dean Dillon seem far less intimidating. Patton also boxed in Phi Delta Theta's

Phi Delt Theta's Slugfest (an intramural boxing competition between four fraternities for charity at UF) for four consecutive years. I believe this is where Bob first heard about the legend of Patton Youngblood. In his senior year, Phi Delta Theta's didn't have a heavyweight contender. Weighing just 185 pounds, Patton knocked out his two opponents to win his weight class and then proceeded to knock out two heavier opponents to win the heavyweight class as well. If you can knock out four opponents in one night, you can handle Dean Dillon's "whatcha gonna do about that" without breaking a sweat.

Patton lived on campus, and since I lived in North St. Pete, I would often hang out in his dorm room between classes. Law school was stressful, but Patton had a way of keeping things light. He could recall every funny line from a movie and loved mimicking the actors. One of our favorites at the time was Eddie Murphy, known for his roles in 48 Hours, Trading Places, and Beverly Hills Cop, as well as his stand-up comedy. We often listened to Eddie's "Delirious", which remains the funniest stand-up set I've ever heard. Lines like "Roll Eddie around, he'll be alright" and "Goonie GOO" left us laughing so hard that our stomachs hurt. What stress? We would have "Patton dogs" for lunch (chili dogs) and sometimes "Patton fish" (tuna fish sandwiches). Patton has built a successful plaintiff's practice in Tampa and St. Pete over the years, and we remain close friends.

We also knew it was a game, and hey, we had been playing games our whole lives. Intramurals at Stetson were played on what was fondly known as "Sandspur Field." It wasn't exactly Field of Dreams material, but to each class, it was important. We played football in the fall and softball in the spring. Our summer class had some pretty good athletes, including Patton, Andy Tsafares, Greg Kino, and Lori Brown, who had played softball at Stetson during undergrad. She and I made a solid double-play combo in those days. The fall '87 class right behind us featured a "Hefty Lefty" quarterback (think of University of Kentucky and New York Giants QB Jared Lorenzen) named Jay Hebert. Yes, he was a distant cousin of NFL Saints QB Bobby Hebert and would become my second-best friend from law school. We competed, sometimes not so amicably, on Sandspur Field, but our class team routinely defeated the fall '87ers. Thankfully, there was no intramural swimming because Jay's background was not in football or baseball but as an all-American swimmer who had competed in the Olympic Trials for the 1980 Olympics (which the U.S. boycotted).

Jay swam at LSU for a year and then at Clemson for three years, where he met his wife Terry, a swimmer from Toronto, Canada.

When fall classes started in 1987, the new students had to take Contracts with Cal Kuenzel. Jay joked that it was almost back to the Peabody Hotel for him— because he had worked there before law school, famous for their ducks, in Houston. Fortunately, he passed Kuenzel's class and continued on. Jay didn't have Dean Dillon for Real Property, which he reminded us about whenever we complained about Dillon. Patton, Jay, and I all had Torts I with Mickey Smiley that fall. We caught a break with Mickey, realizing we could get through Torts without reading and briefing all the cases. Mickey taught directly from Legalines, a case brief summary publication that identified the issue, rule, analysis, and conclusion (IRAC). With that simplified approach, we were on our way to graduating law school. I later learned that Jay had gone to elementary, middle, and high school with some of my best friends from Kappa Sigma: Benton Wood, Dave <u>H</u>enley, and Ken Cooper. It was quite a small-world moment for Jay and me when we discovered that we would both be going to the S&H tournament, a golf event Dave organized with one of Jay's best friends from high school, Steve <u>S</u>chofield.

Jay and I cemented our lifelong friendship in my last semester of law school in the fall of 1989. We both signed up for the public defender's clinic and became trial partners. The clinic provided students the chance to handle real cases for the public defender while still in school. We had clients, some of whom couldn't afford bail and remained in jail. We conducted client interviews at the jail, researched case law, crime scene investigations, witness interviews, pretrial motions, and prepared for and conducted trials before a jury or judge. It was pretty heady stuff for soon-to-be lawyers, but we weren't alone—we were supervised by a professor and an assistant public defender. In total, we handled five cases that semester, and, as we like to say, were the only trial team undefeated that semester. That's right—we "won" all five cases! A record that still stands today, or so we claim!

We even had a Perry Mason moment in one of the trials. The arresting officer was on the stand, being questioned by the prosecutor. As part of our trial strategy, we had gone to Goodwill to get our client a suit. Jay sat at one end of the table, I was next to him, our client sat next to me, and our supervising attorney was at the far end. When the critical part of the testimony came where the officer had to identify the defendant, he mistakenly identified our not-so-sharply dressed assistant public defender (in a brown coat with patches on the elbows) as the defendant—not once but twice: the officer said, "No, I mean yes, the one at the end of the table with the brown patches on his jacket." Jay and I immediately stood and, in unison, requested the judge grant "one of those

JNOVs…umm…we mean directed verdicts" for the defense, which the judge promptly granted. VICTORY!

# Chapter 5

# My Work Family

*" I don't get it Mike, those guys from North Palm Beach won't tell me yes or no on an offer. They just keep stringing me along" I said.*

*" That terrible", Mike replied. "You've clerked here for two years and everybody has seen you are a hard worker, why don't you come to work for us."*

*"Because you haven't ask me to!" I nearly begged. He said he would get with the other partners and let me know by Friday if I had a job.*

*Friday Morning Mike called, " I have an offer…"*

*"I'll take it!" I interrupted, not waiting for the details.*

### *Lyle and Skipper, P.A.*

Since the fall of 1987, I had been clerking for Lyle & Skipper, P.A., an insurance defense firm in St. Petersburg. Although academics were not going to secure me a job after school, I believed that experience and confidence could help me land something. L&S was a fifty-year-old firm founded by Mr. Lyle and had an excellent reputation. The office was located in an old bank building just outside of downtown, and the library, where the clerks worked, was housed in the former bank vault. My duties included conducting research, writing memorandums, and occasionally attending hearings and depositions. Before my final semester of law school in the fall of 1989, I wanted to broaden my horizons, so I sought and accepted a summer clerkship in North Palm Beach with the insurance defense firm DeSantis Cook, P.A. This is the last time I will ever mention their name.

I remember two things about this experience. First, I subleased an apartment from a young woman with very long black hair. She must have had an abundance of it because it was everywhere in her room, particularly embedded in the white carpet of the bathroom. Now, I am far from being Mr. Clean (remember the rats), but this was unsettling. No matter how hard I tried, I could not remove all the hair.

Secondly, after the summer ended, I inquired about a job. I was told they would discuss it and get back to me. After returning to school, I followed up several more times and was repeatedly told that it was still being discussed. To this day, I am still waiting for their decision. Bad form—and no, I am not over it. It would have been fine if they cut me; after all, I had been cut twice from my high school baseball team. But receiving no response at all was unacceptable. Whenever I interviewed someone I always gave them the courtesy of answer even if it was "no."

In December 1989, I graduated magna cum nada from Stetson College of Law. I had a job offer from the Public Defender (5–0, BABY!). At least I wasn't heading back to Miami to practice with my father, but I really didn't want to do criminal work—I had always envisioned myself as a big-shot CIVIL TRIAL lawyer. A few weeks before graduation, I met Mike Kiernan for lunch. I mentioned to Mike, with whom I had worked closely at Lyle & Skipper as a law clerk, that I was disappointed not to have heard back from the defense firm in NPB and that I would likely be taking the Public Defender job. Mike asked, "Why don't you work for us?" I replied, "Because you haven't offered me a job." He took it to his partners, and within 48 hours, I had a job offer: starting salary $28,000 before passing the bar, bumped up to $30,000 once I passed. Woohoo—I could finally afford a place without RATS!

I primarily worked for Mike, who handled a mix of general liability and worker's compensation defense, and for Bob Byelick, who focused solely on worker's compensation defense. I've always said I had the best of both worlds as mentors. Mike was almost reckless with the responsibilities he gave me. He would hand me an assignment or a case file and let me figure it out on my own. One time, he sent me to interview witnesses at their apartment. I arrived around 10 a.m., and it seemed like they either had a massive party the night before or always partied hard. I suspect the latter. When I woke the household from their slumber, let's just say the interviews did not go well. Bob, on the other hand, was always there if I needed help. He would micromanage me through assignments—not a bad thing for someone who knew very little at the time.

I passed the Florida Bar Exam on the first try and was sworn in by my dad on May 5, 1990, at the Thompson Family reunion in Ft. Myers. I was on my way, and I think my dad was pretty proud of me. The opportunity to swear me in as a member of the Florida Bar was the icing on the cake.

But as college football great Lee Corso would say, "Not so fast, my friend." In January 1991, just short of my one-year anniversary as a lawyer, I was invited to lunch with Bob and Mike. Something felt off, and my initial thought was that I was being fired. It turned out there was indeed an issue, but fortunately, my first instinct was wrong. Mike and Bob were leaving Lyle & Skipper and wanted me to join them. WHAT? Apart from that unmentionable firm in NPB, L&S was all I knew. There were many great lawyers at L&S, they had recently opened an office in Tampa, and I had dreams of moving there soon. And, oh yeah, what about the files? That was up to the clients, but Mike and Bob were confident most would follow them—or so they told me and their new partners. The partners at L&S tried to keep me. I wasn't naive enough to think it was about me personally, but they needed someone to handle their worker's compensation files if they wanted to retain those clients. With the two main attorneys leaving, the rookie was their best option.

### *Fox and Grove*

I met with the primary partners at the new firm, Fox and Grove. The main partner, David Abbey, misunderstood my name, and it became a running joke. He thought my name was "Lou Davici," leading to my new nickname: "LOUJOE." I didn't care what he called me; what mattered to me was their "bonus" compensation program. A recently promoted partner and former associate, Brian Reynolds, explained: for every hour I billed over two thousand hours per year, I would receive a twenty-five-dollar-per-hour bonus. CONFIDENCE! I was not only trained by two excellent substantive lawyers but also by THE two best billing lawyers in the world.

Billable hours: the lifeblood of an insurance defense lawyer. If you don't write it down, the insurance company won't pay you. They were already paying a fraction of other lawyers' hourly rate, noted. So the only way to keep the RATS at bay was to bill every .1 (or 6 minutes) of every hour worked. And if you worked smart, you could bill more than the actual hours worked.

Let me illustrate I have a deposition of an injured worker at 2 p.m. in Tampa. I leave by 1:00 p.m. to arrive downtown well before 2, allow for traffic delays, greet the other lawyer, use the restroom, get coffee, etc. In the morning, I work on my files and ignore phone calls. As I leave, I pick up my pink phone message slips. While exiting the garage, I start returning calls on my new "car" phone, billing each call at a minimum of fifteen minutes. I bill forty-five minutes for travel to Tampa, one hour for the deposition, and then dictate my deposition summary letter to the client on my handheld Dictaphone on the way back to the office. I'm back by 3:45—no need to be early, just on time. I bill client A two and a half hours for travel and the deposition, 0.7 for the deposition summary, and 0.3 for calls to clients B, C, and D. Two and a half hours worked, three and a half hours billed. Processing mail (and it doesn't take six minutes to read a two-page letter and dictate a response) might mean two hours worked, three and a half hours billed. It wasn't easy, but with hard work and diligence, it could be done.

I didn't need to work eighty hours a week to bill fifty; I could work forty-five hours and easily bill fifty. Arrive at the office by 8:00 a.m., take an ½ hour for lunch, leave by 6:00 p.m., and be home with the kids by 6:30. Working fifty weeks a year (because I needed my two weeks' vacation), I could bill an extra five hundred bonus hours at twenty-five dollars per hour—an additional $12,500 per year. A salary bump to $32,000 plus the bonus was worth the risk of joining the new firm. All I needed were the files. One hundred "good" cases, and I'd be a star. CONFIDENCE!

I made the move to Fox and Grove with Bob and Mike, and the cases followed us. The only downside was that I would now be a full-time worker's compensation attorney (with only judge/bench trials). My dream of being a civil trial lawyer making grand arguments to a jury would not materialize. Still, it was worth it. I would be financially secure—not rich—but I could have a family life, which was very important to me. Did I mention no evening or weekend work? Not many lawyers can say that.

Two other associates Dick Gurley and Joe Mueller made practicing law fun. Dick was one of the funniest guys I ever met. Dick was from Chicago and he would often call to grab lunch at Mike's Deli on Ulmerton Road. Their specialty was Chicago Beef and sausage on a hoagie roll. His call about going to lunch would start with "sausage one to sausage two, come in". I always knew we were in for a good lunch. Dick was an Irish American but he often said he was "Italian by ingestion." If it had been a tough day, I could always go into Dick's office and get a good laugh. We talked often about leaving the practice of law and moving to Europe. We called these our Belgium days. I'm not sure why as neither of us had a connection to Belgium.

Joe Mueller was not as funny as Dick, but when he came on board after Dick left the firm, he became my sanity check. Not surprisingly, I could get pretty worked up about my cases. Inevitably, I would dictate a harsh letter to a dumb client or opposing attorney and when I got it back from transcription at least I was smart enough to take it to Joe to have him review it. He would tone it down for me and that saved a lot of clients and cases

from blowing up.

I excelled at Fox and Grove. I was consistently among the top 1 or 2 lawyers in the firm in billable hours. In 1996, I was invited to become a partner, which is the ultimate goal for any associate at a law firm. After becoming a partner, I hired an associate, Chris Petrucelli. Chris was a bulldog, and I not only taught him the substantive law of worker's compensation but also all the billing lessons I learned from Mike and Bob. He thrived. Once Chris was established, I hired a second associate, Kelly Fisher. Kelly was smart, diligent, and proved to be a tremendous asset to the firm. By 2000, I was a partner with my own caseload, supervising two associates, two paralegals, and a legal assistant. I had also just welcomed my second child, Ashlyn. Other than the commute to St. Petersburg, things were going well—both financially and in my law practice.

# Chapter 6

# My Married-Into Family

*"But Professor she signed the contract; I think it should be enforced". I argued.*

*"But they repossessed all her furniture even though she had more than paid for several items. Professor Swigert fumed. Well, no one forced her to sign the contract, there was not coercion or misrepresentation."*

*I countered not giving ground. "You, you... macho race car driver", he proclaimed.*

### *Lorena May Hart*

My connection to my married-into family began in law school. When I started at Stetson in the summer of 1987, our class had fifty-three students, marking the first time Stetson's incoming class had more women than men—a trend that, I believe, continues to this day. As I mentioned before, we started with three classes that summer semester: Research and Writing I with Professor Armstrong, Contracts with the occasionally "slightly off" Professor Swigert, and Real Property with Dean "what ya gonna do about that" Dillon. In law school, the entire grade for a class hinges on the final exam at the end of the semester. A lot of pressure. Our first exam was in Real Property. Dean Dillon warned us that we needed to obtain our exam numbers from the registrar before the exam. All exams were anonymous, and if we forgot, we wouldn't be able to get our numbers until he finished the pre-exam instructions and the clock had started ticking. We had two hours to complete the exam.

As Dillon was about halfway through his instructions, a pretty blonde in the front row raised her hand in a panic and said, "I don't have my number." Dean Dillon, calm and somewhat cruel, finished his instructions at a measured pace, started the clock, and then allowed her to leave the room. She dashed to the registrar's office and returned after everyone else had been working on the exam for about 15 minutes. I felt a little sorry for her, but my friend Mike Trentalange had a theory about rocks: some people in law school were going to swim, and some were going to sink like rocks. It didn't matter how well you swam, as long as you reached the edge of the pool. At that moment, I figured I had a better chance than she did of making it to the pool edge.

In the fall semester, we had Contracts II with Swigert. He remained temperamental, and early in the semester, he became irritated when the same pretty blonde couldn't explain the difference between "consideration" and "estoppel." He told her she'd better know the difference by the end of the semester. Ah…the rock was sinking. Or so I thought. I was wrong about that.

Later that semester, she began to take notice of me. For that, I owe a nod to Swigert.

One day, Professor Swigert was in one of his infamous moods (later, I hope, diagnosed and treated medically), and I was in his sight, or at least one of his targets. We were discussing a case involving a little old Black lady and a rent-to-own furniture store. The case name still sticks with me: <u>Williams v. Walker Furniture Store</u>. The woman had been buying the furniture on credit, but when she made her monthly payments as per the contract, only part of the payment went toward the first pieces she had purchased. When she defaulted, the store repossessed all her furniture, even though she had paid more than enough for some of the pieces. The appellate court ruled the contract was "unconscionable", meaning it was so unfair that it was unenforceable. I argued that the woman had signed the contract with full disclosure of its terms, so it should be enforced.

Professor Swigert and I had a spirited debate (much like the ones I had over dinner with my brother and dad), until he grew flustered. With sweat glistening on his reddened face, he shouted, "You, you...macho race car driver!" I'm still not sure what he meant by that, but I suspect he was calling me insensitive. Regardless, the pretty blonde turned around from her front-row seat and noticed that I **WAS** indeed pretty "macho," a trait she found appealing.

## Why I am Who I Am                    Joseph P. Ludovici

An interesting sidelight during law school: Ludovici, being a rare name, always stands out once people learn it. While at Stetson, I received a call from Peter Ludovici. He was visiting St. Pete Beach and had seen my listing in the phone book. He and his wife invited me over to meet them. I accepted, and of course, in Italian tradition, I had to be fed—salami, cheese, and a little red wine. I learned they were from West Virginia and that their family had immigrated to Canada before moving to the U.S. Peter didn't know where his family was originally from in Italy, as they had immigrated in the late 1800s. Although we didn't find a familial connection, it was wonderful meeting them. Ironically, they had a son, a little older than me, also named Joseph, who was a practicing attorney in Illinois. Another one of those small-world occurrences.

Since our class was close-knit due to its size, we often went out and partied together. I got to know the pretty blonde better, and in March, I needed a date. My brother was coming to Tampa with his wife, Sue, and wanted to eat at Tampa's premier steakhouse, Bern's. I had never been there and only knew it was expensive. I asked my brother if I could bring a date and made sure he was footing the bill—he is very generous with his money. I mentioned to my friend John Guyton from Tampa that I was going to Bern's and needed a date. The blonde and I disagree about where this conversation took place. I believe it was by the pool at Stetson, where she called out, "I'll go with you to Bern's." She insists it happened in the library, which I doubt, given how little time I spent there during law school (my grades, while not "rock" level, reflect this). Regardless of the location, we both agree she invited herself to Bern's, and who could blame her—it's a five-star steakhouse.

For the date she wore a form-fitting leopard print dress with the back cut out. Whenever I touched her bare skin, I would immediately draw my hand back. She thought this was cute given my nervousness. The date went great except for when she tried the Caviar. She was unaware that it was fish roe and she did not eat fish. I think she took a big sip of wine and forced it down. At dinner she realized I was the soft-spoken brother but she held her own with Ed.

A few weeks later, when she learned I wasn't going home for Easter, she invited me to her family's Easter gathering at Lake Tarpon with her parents. That made two dates she invited me on, and now I am meeting the family. Sounded a bit desperate to me. I went, and it was fine, except I started off by lying to her mom. She asked if I had gone to church that Easter morning, and I said yes. I didn't. In fact, I hadn't been to church regularly since leaving home for college. I confessed this lie to her mom years later and asked for forgiveness. After Easter, we began seeing each other but kept it private. Stetson was a small community, and we didn't want our business to be public. Our first official date that I asked her out on was windsurfing with our friends Jay and Terry Hebert over Memorial Day weekend. A new tradition was begun – spending Memorial Day with the Heberts. It was a disaster. I have never had strong upper-body strength and could never do enough pull-ups as a kid to earn the President's Award for fitness. I couldn't windsurf. Not even for a few seconds. I was cursing and beyond frustrated. I fancied myself an athlete, but this was a sport I would never master. I don't think the pretty blonde was impressed by my performance, and I know she wasn't thrilled by my expletives. Sadly, she witnessed plenty more of that on Sand Spur Field over the next couple of years. COCKINESS, more so than confidence!

As the semester drew to a close, we were studying for finals. We decided to form a study group at her apartment, joined by Patton Youngblood and the pretty blonde's roommate, John McCorvey, who was also a Summer '87 Stetson student. After we finished studying, the plan was for me to go downstairs with Patton, pretend to leave, and then come back upstairs to spend time with her. I said goodbye to Patton, got in my car, but never drove out of the parking lot. Instead, I went back upstairs to hang out with the pretty blonde.

The next day, Patton and I were sitting near the Publix in Gulfport after getting ice cream. We sat on a telephone pole lying on the ground with a few other friends—Jay, John, and Ken

Turkel. That telephone pole became known as the "log of truth" because, that day, Patton confronted me. He said he had waited for me at the parking lot exit and wanted to know why I hadn't driven out. Jay stayed silent as he had promised.  Oops, I was busted. I told him I had left through the other driveway. No good—he knew there was only one driveway. I had to come clean and admit that I was seeing Lorena May Hart, the pretty blonde. She wasn't thrilled that our cover was blown but got over it pretty quickly.

It turned out she was far from a "sinking rock." She had graduated from the University of Florida in just three and a half years with a business degree and graduated from Stetson Law with Honors. She was one of only three students to earn an A in Professor Swigert's Contracts II class. So, she figured out "consideration" and plenty of other legal theories. That same semester, she also earned the highest grade on the midterm in Criminal Pro I. She was diligent and studied very hard, often helping me with my studies. I had to return the favor at times, like when I was teaching her constitutional law the night before the exam. Constitutional law is the closest thing to a history class in law school, so I was confident in it. The next day, she got an A while I earned a B+. That was frustrating!

Being a good writer was important, and she certainly was skilled in that area. We dated throughout law school, and when it came time for the bar exam, she was unstoppable. By then, she was living in North St. Pete, but we would both be at the USF St. Pete College Library by 8 a.m., studying straight through until at least 8 p.m. We'd usually head back to my apartment, where she'd stay up for another two or three hours studying while I vegged out on the couch watching sports. All the hard work and preparation paid off—we both passed the bar exam on the first try. Although the exam is pass/fail, they do provide your score. And yes, in case you're wondering (and I'm definitely glad to tell you): I got a better score than she did. I just needed her to push me to study as hard as we did. That effort, which my parents always hoped to see from me, proved to be the key to my bar exam success.

When Lorena was looking for a job, she came across a firm that specialized exclusively in eminent domain law. Neither of us knew what that entailed, but I encouraged her to send her résumé. She did, and soon interviewed with the main partner in Tampa, Cary Gaylord. It was his first interview for a new associate, and he planned to visit other law schools, like the University of Florida, to meet more candidates. We soon learned that eminent domain is the government's power to take private property for public projects such as roads and schools, with the requirement to pay "just" compensation. Lawyers who represent property owners earn a percentage of the increase they secure for their clients over the government's initial offer. It's a litigation-heavy practice, which wasn't exactly Lorena's initial goal, she had wanted a career in real estate/transactional law. But with the Savings and Loan crisis in just swing, real estate wasn't a viable option. Cary offered her the job, and she accepted. Although she originally aimed to be a real estate transactional lawyer, not a litigator, it turned out to be the right decision. Lorena has been with Cary for the past thirty-five years, litigating significant cases and achieving great success, both financially and professionally. I did well as an insurance defense attorney, but we were confined to hourly rates. Lorena's practice, on the other hand, resembled that of a plaintiff's personal injury practice, with high stakes and big rewards. I've always told people that not only was she "the smart lawyer in the family," but also "the rich one."

Lorena's strong work ethic came from her parents, Fred J. Hart and Mary Alice Gannon Hart, who are some of the best in-laws a guy could ask for. Fred was always willing to help with any project, whether it was re-piping the Dana Shores house or pouring a concrete patio around the grey house. An electrical engineer by education and training, Fred owned his own business as a manufacturing representative for global companies that sold machines for bending and forming metals. He worked in the industry for over 40 years, traveling throughout Florida after moving the family to Tampa in 1980. Mary was a homemaker and only twenty when she had Lorena. Lorena has two younger sisters: Robin, who is five years younger, and Mary Beth, who is ten years younger. Mary is an excellent cook, and my favorite dish of hers is her macaroni and cheese.

Fred and Mary were both born and raised in southern Ohio, just across the Ohio River from Huntington, West Virginia—Fred from Chesapeake and Mary from Southpoint. They came from large families, and many of Fred's siblings eventually settled in Tampa. Mary would host Christmas and Easter dinners with the extended family, and they were always fun gatherings. One tradition I never fully understood involved a large wax candle. It was an odd, eclectic item that was given as a gag gift every Christmas and passed around year after year. I often wonder what happened to that candle.

While Lorena and I were dating, her parents' dog, Gidget, had puppies. Lorena wanted one but, since she was living in an apartment and working full-time, she decided she needed two— Trinket and Tike. When we got married, they became our dogs, and we decided to breed Trinket. I was fully on board because Lorena assured me that we could sell multiple pups for at least $300 each, as they were papered toy poodles. It didn't go as planned. Trinket only had one puppy, and, of course, I fell in love with her. That's how Tigger joined the clan. The image of Mr. "Macho Race Car Driver" with three toy poodles was amusing to me. They slept in our bed, and I would often wake up to find one nestled in each armpit and one between my legs. Fred and Mary were excellent "grandparents" to these dogs and would puppy-sit whenever needed. When we had children and the dogs aged, Fred and Mary took them in and dealt with their passing when the time came. It worked out pretty well for us.

Before we were married on March 7, 1992, we bought our first home in Dana Shores, located just west of the airport in Tampa on a canal that leads to Tampa Bay. We really stretched to buy the house, but following the advice of Lorena's partner, Kim Merlin, we overreached. We were so far in debt that we couldn't afford to replace the carpet, which usually wouldn't be a problem, but the previous owners were smokers and drinkers—a risky proposition. The carpet had hundreds of cigarette burns, some as long as three inches. It's amazing the house never caught fire. At least there were no rats—or so I thought!

About nine months after we moved in, the water line leading into the house ruptured beneath the concrete floor in the laundry room. We had no money to hire a plumber, but fortunately, we had Lorena's father, Fred, and our new neighbor, Robert Polans, to help. We rerouted the water throughout the house from the attic, which meant spending a lot of time up there in July. At one point, I thought I had killed my father-in-law—not an experience I'd recommend in the first year of marriage. He came down from the attic and collapsed on the garage floor for what felt like an eternity.

**Why I am Who I Am** — **Joseph P. Ludovici**

Thankfully, he recovered, and after a long weekend, we had running water again.

The wedding reception was a blast. Fred could fix anything around the house, but he was also an exceptional hillbilly dancer. There was a lot of dancing at the reception, and soon everyone's shoes ended up in a pile in the middle of the dance floor. Fred and my dad led the way, shoes and socks off, pants rolled up to their knees, tugging on their suspender straps, and kicking up their heels. Fred was from Boo-boo Holler' in Chesapeake, Ohio, so I knew he had it in him, but I wasn't sure where my dad picked up those moves. I guess jitterbugging translates well to hillbilly dancing.

This was supposed to be a dignified affair. We had rented the Tampa Club on the forty-first and forty-second floors of the Bank of America building in downtown Tampa, complete with a full buffet and open bar for about 150 guests. Everyone showed up, and when the bartender offered to make frozen drinks like daiquiris and piña coladas, people eagerly accepted. We blew the budget on the bar tab, but it was worth it, even if it did contribute to the reception's lively—and slightly chaotic—atmosphere. Along with the shoeless hillbilly dancing, Lorena's Uncle Paul added plastic flies to the wedding cake. This was fine with Lorena because her vision for the cake hadn't turned out as planned. She wanted a strawberry-filled cake from Publix with buttercream icing, and

171

while it tasted delicious, the flower decorations were a dull, brownish color instead of the vibrant hues she envisioned. The plastic flies actually livened up the look.

After the wedding, Lorena moved into the house in Dana Shores. She hadn't moved in when we bought it because we weren't married, and I didn't want to upset my mom by "living in sin." Due to our financial situation, we kept roommates. Lorena's middle sister, Robin, lived with me before the wedding, and when she moved out, my friend Bobby Shaw moved in. The rent we collected from Robin and Bobby helped us pay the mortgage and allowed us to get new carpeting. Bobby stayed for a couple of years until we needed his room for the baby's nursery.

Dana Shores was a great house, with a canal leading to Tampa Bay and a nice pool and hot tub. When Andrew Hebert was just two we continued our Memorial Day tradition and had the Hebert's over for a BBQ and pool party. We were in the hot tub when Andrew suddenly jumped out, stood next to the bushes, pulled down his swimsuit, and peed. His parents, both swimmers, had taught him well – NO peeing in the pool.

In Dana Shores, we lived right next to Chrissy and Robert Polans. Robert had grown up in Miami and went to my rival high school, Killian, an instant connection. They had both graduated from UF a few years after us, and we became very close. Our kitchen window faced their house, and when Lorena and I would eat "dinner"—which often meant standing at the kitchen sink eating chips and salsa—they would call us over for a proper meal. Every weekend, we decided who would cook and whose house would host "movie night." Living on a canal with access to the bay, Robert and I both owned Aquasports, open fisherman boats, and we spent a lot of time out on the water together. Chrissy was an attorney, and Robert worked as a drug rep for Johnson & Johnson. In 1992, we decided to buy season tickets for the Gator games together and still have those tickets today.

One of the funniest stories they tell is when we went to McDonald's to get hamburgers. They were having a special, and they were 39¢. Robert Chrissy and I all ordered hamburgers. Lorena ordered cheeseburgers. The guy on the mic said, "Ma'am, those are not on special. They are the regular price of $1.29." Lorena ordered them anyway. When I questioned her frugality, she gave a classic Lorena rely: "I choose the profession I choose, so I could have cheese on my hamburger." To hell with the fact that a slice of cheese cost 90¢.

Unfortunately, as Robert advanced in his career, they had to move out of state. He kept the Gator tickets, which we made good use of as our kids got older. Chrissy stayed home with their two children, Morgan and Zach, after they moved. Fortunately, about eight years ago, they moved back to Florida and built a beautiful home in Ormond Beach. We've shared some great Florida vs.

Georgia weekends with them and hope to spend more time with them, especially since Morgan, now an attorney, lives in Tampa with her new baby girl, Luna. Tragically, they lost Zach last year, which has been incredibly difficult for them. We've supported them as best we can.

Lorena grew up tent camping with her parents and uncles, visiting places like Myrtle Beach, South Carolina, Louisiana, the Smoky Mountains, and Florida. On one trip, they arrived at a picturesque campground in the Florida Keys on a holiday weekend, surprised to find it nearly empty. They soon discovered why: as the sun set, swarms of mosquitoes descended on their campsite, prompting them to pack up and move the next morning. I'm fairly certain this was Big Pine Campground where we camped a lot of summers. At least I know the mosquitoes were just as lethal.

Given my childhood camping experiences, I wasn't thrilled when Lorena planned a tent trip to Cades Cove in the Smoky Mountains of North Carolina with her parents. She promised cool mountain weather and no bugs but failed to mention that it was rustic camping with no electricity or running water (i.e., no showers or flush toilets). She also didn't mention that it was in a rainforest. It rained often, and the only place to clean up was in a mountain spring. It was freezing, but after two days of an upset stomach, I had to take a "bath." That's when I earned the nickname "SBJ" (Sh@&ty Butt Joe).

When our kids came along, Lorena wanted them to experience camping too. We tent camped for a few years until JoJo was born. When he was about a year old, we went to a Gator game and then camped just outside of Gainesville. It was October but got so cold that Lorena had to sleep with JoJo on her chest to keep him from freezing. After that, I insisted on no more tent camping. We bought a pop-up trailer. It had a heater, and, more importantly, an air conditioner. I joked that I bought an air conditioner that just happened to come with a camper.

In 1998, we sold the Dana Shores house and moved to Odessa in Northwest Hillsborough County. Lorena was working on eminent domain cases for the Veterans Expressway at the time and liked the area, known for its ski lakes. Back in the day, this was where South Tampanians had their weekend and summer lake houses. Lorena found a beautiful, oak-filled property with a three-story A-frame house in one corner. The property had a long driveway and a small wooden bridge to cross to reach the house. The bonus was that there was space for another house near the big ski lake, Lake Josephine. We planned to stay in the "grey" house for just a couple of years before building on the other part of the lot. The three-story house, with the master bedroom on the top floor, kept us fit—no need for a Stairmaster. In 2003, we built the "yellow" house. Building a house is always challenging, but it's even harder when you live on the property and see the progress (or lack thereof) every day.

To build our new house, we needed access to the lot through our neighbors' property to the north. We asked Glen and Karen Carty if we could bring dump trucks and concrete trucks across their land. They graciously agreed with only one condition: they wanted a specific oak limb to remain untouched because they planned to hang a swing from it when they built their house. Unfortunately, during the first week of construction, the superintendent cut off the limb and attempted to cover it up by painting it black and draping Spanish moss over it. To say we got off to a bad start would be an understatement. Amazingly, Glen and Karen have remained our neighbors for 20 years and even rented the "grey" house while their own home was being built next door. I think they might finally forgive us next year for cutting their tree limb off.

### *Alexis Nicole Ludovici*

We weren't sure if the nursery would ever be needed in Dana Shores. We began trying to have a baby in 1993, but after no success the old-fashioned way, even with Lorena on Clomid, we eventually had to try artificial insemination. Now, I was the "six-million-dollar" man—I had stronger swimmers than the women's

East German swim team in the 1980s. Unfortunately, they weren't reaching their destination, so we needed expert help. The process involved me going to the doctor's office in Tampa first thing in the morning to make my "delivery." It wasn't too bad; the restroom had plenty of prompting material, and I'd been practicing since I was about thirteen. I dropped off my package at the front desk and jokingly told the receptionist to be careful with my child. She either didn't get the joke or had heard it too many times to find it funny. I laughed all the way to St. Pete. After spinning the raw material, the doctor met with Lorena in the afternoon for the "turkey baster" treatment. We had to go through this process multiple times, and I always tell people that, unlike the movies we watched in junior high, there's more than one way to conceive a baby. I wasn't even in the same county as Lorena when conception happened.

Alexis Nicole was born on July 11, 1996, 7-Eleven. I joked about naming her Slurpee, but that idea didn't go over well, so we settled on Alexis. We considered Alexandria, but with Ludovici as her last name, we worried her full name wouldn't fit into the squares on a credit card application when she grew up. Like all parents say, Alexis was a beautiful baby. Her blue-grey eyes were captivating, and complete strangers at church or the mall would ask if they could hold her, which was a bit unsettling. People constantly remarked on her beauty. She even made it into print: a photo taken when she was about nine months old was used by the photographer in a Bealls department store ad for picture frames. When Alexis was two, we entered her in a pageant. We brought her Christmas dress, only to realize we were outmatched by the elaborate outfits of other contestants. But that didn't matter. Alexis was confident on stage and did a great job. When it came time for the awards, we were a bit disappointed when she wasn't named one of the three runners-up. Then they announced the winner: Alexis had won! She was a beautiful baby and has grown into a beautiful young lady. She always loved the stage and became an accomplished competitive dancer in high school.

Alexis was also an excellent student. When she earned straight A's in sixth grade, we agreed she could get a puppy. Reese's, named after the candy bar, was light and dark brown when she was born, resembling a Reese's Cup. Reese's was a Soft-Coated Wheaten Terrier, a working dog breed that turned the color of wheat by her first year, but the name stuck. She was part of our family for 15 years and adored by the kids. Bred to herd, Reese's would chase the kids around the family room, playfully nipping at their butts and heels to "corral" them. She loved hiking in the North Carolina mountains and never strayed far from me when I was working in my home office. She would often lie at my feet under the desk, and I was heartbroken when we decided it was time to put her down. In her last weeks, she became disoriented and suffered greatly, so we had to make the difficult decision. Laps of Love came to the house while Ashlyn and JoJo were home from college. Grandma joined us, and Alexis was on FaceTime. It was a peaceful and beautiful transition.

Alexis was not very interested in playing sports. She played soccer when she was young but would hide behind the light pole when I tried to get her onto the field for practice. I was her coach, and one night she told me she didn't want to play anymore. She quickly corrected herself to say she didn't want to play anymore for ME as her coach. I was a bit overzealous in my coaching style. It's a good thing she didn't take to soccer because she found her true passion in dance. She danced with her best friend, Casey Seguiti, at Dance Makers under Ms. Nan and Ms. Collete. Alexis made many close friends there, and when she was old enough, she began competing. We traveled all over Central Florida for dance competitions, and I even became a "Dancing Dad."

At the end of the school year, Dance Makers held a big production, and Alexis would dance in six to eight numbers. For some comedic relief, the dads would also perform a routine. Unlike my parents, the stage was not my friend. Fred Seguiti and I danced for about five years, and we were terrible. I couldn't remember the steps, which gave me a newfound respect for Alexis and her friends. Alexis performed flawlessly in multiple styles of dances, except once—while en pointe, she suddenly crumbled. But she got right back up, her beautiful smile never fading, and she finished the performance. She definitely has the perseverance gene.

*One side note about RATS! While we were at the hospital having Alexis, a rat got into the dryer vent and climbed into the dryer. When we returned home, something smelled terrible in the laundry room, which connected the garage to the house. I couldn't really smell it, and I attributed Lorena's heightened sense of smell to being a new mother. I ignored her concerns, and in the excitement of bringing Alexis home, it was a couple more days in the searing July heat before I noticed the familiar smell and knew immediately what was wrong. After a quick search, I found the source and didn't even try to clean it out. I dragged the dryer out to the street for the garbage pickup and bought a new one. Problem solved. Man, I HATE RATS!

Alexis is my "Italian" child. Like my dad, I have both American kids and an Italian kid. For her 16th birthday, Alexis wanted to invite her dance friends to Disney World for a princess experience. She also wanted to serve them Polenta "su la Tavola," an Italian cornmeal dish served on a communal table—or in our case, a plywood board. My brother had made Alexis her own board, and we brought it to Orlando. The girls loved it. The dish is simple: cornmeal with pasta "gravy" poured over it, meatballs, sausage, and salad. No dishes are used—everything is served directly on the board. It was a family tradition we enjoyed often with my dad's Italian friends in Miami, especially the Capuas and Romanos.

After graduating from Steinbrenner High School in Tampa, Alexis applied to several SEC schools for college. She wanted the full SEC college football experience. She was accepted everywhere she applied but particularly liked Missouri, Georgia, and UF. I had made the mistake of taking her on visits to several SEC schools during her senior year, which included an epic football weekend. We visited Ole Miss in Oxford, Mississippi, and participated in "rushing to the Grove" on Friday night, a great college football tradition where tailgaters secure their spots on the main campus lawn, "the Grove," at 5:01 p.m. We explored the Grove the next morning and met the Flying Elvises of Ole Miss fame. We watched the 12:30 p.m. game against Arkansas and then drove to Tuscaloosa, Alabama, to watch Alabama play LSU that night in a classic showdown. Not many sixteen- or seventeen-year-old girls would be excited to watch two college football games in one day, but Alexis was all in. Later, we took a road trip to Missouri, which was another highlight. We got to party with Andrew Hebert (Jay's son) and his friends, giving her a taste of real college life. Playing Slam and Bunnies with Mr. Jay (Hebert) was a hoot.

UF was the last school to announce admissions, and when they accepted Alexis, her mom and I were ecstatic and expected her to

181

be overjoyed. After all, she had been a Gator her whole life. She had even attended the UF vs. FSU National Championship Game in New Orleans as a six-month-old. But Alexis remained silent, saying she hadn't made up her mind yet. WHAT? After weeks of waiting for her decision, with deadlines for dorm deposits looming, I told Alexis to put together the pros and cons of attending each of the three schools, and we would meet at five o'clock Friday afternoon to discuss it. Not one for confrontation , on Thursday morning, she asked her mom if, by agreeing to go to UF, could we cancel the Friday meeting? Absolutely! MISSION ACCOMPLISHED! Alexis was going to be a GATOR!

Alexis graduated with a degree in journalism and a minor in Italian Studies. She studied at the University of Perugia in Italy during the spring semester of her junior year and speaks Italian very well. She needed an extra semester (and an extra football season) to complete the Italian Studies minor and knew exactly how to convince me to agree. An Italian Studies degree for my Italian child? Sure, you can stay another semester. That fall, she attended every UF football game, both home and away. After graduating, she took a job with the Augusta GreenJackets, a Single-A baseball team in North Augusta, South Carolina. Alexis didn't particularly like baseball, and when Covid canceled her second season, she started exploring other options. She chose hockey because there are no rain delays, extra innings, or six-day-a-week home stands. She had several options but ultimately accepted a job with the Kansas City Mavericks. Her mom and I would have preferred she chose Charleston, South Carolina, to be closer to home, but that wasn't her plan. She made the right move and has enjoyed KC and the Mavericks. She received numerous compliments from Lamar Hunt Jr., the owner of the Mavericks and part of the KC Chiefs legacy. She even spoke at the ECHL summer meeting about her role with the team. She produces and directs everything about the game, except for the players on the ice. Alexis hopes to continue her career in hockey and move up the league, maybe even to the NHL.

### *Ashlyn Noel Ludovici*

Once Alexis turned one, we started trying for a second child. We tried the old-fashioned way for several months but soon realized we weren't having any success. So, we moved on to artificial insemination, but even after three or four tries, we had no luck. We were getting desperate. Lorena had surgery for endometriosis, but even that didn't work. We decided to switch to another fertility specialist after the first one, who had helped us conceive Alexis, tried to sell us Amway after she was born. I figured if he needed to sell Amway, he might not be the right doctor for us. It took three tries at in-vitro fertilization before Ashlyn was conceived. We were nervous because for the first two tries, we implanted only two fertilized eggs, but the last time, we implanted three. Oh God, we thought, we might have triplets or at least twins. Twins ran in the family; Fred had a twin sister, Betty. Knowing Ashlyn as I do now and watching her play soccer growing up, it's no surprise those other embryos never stood a chance. Despite her small size, she is one tough cookie. I remember her rolling down the stairs in our three-story "grey" house in Odessa. When she landed at the bottom, she looked up at me, and when I showed no reaction, she got up and ran off to wherever she was headed.

Ashlyn Noel was due on Christmas Day but was delivered by caesarean on December 20, 1999. She was breech and has been wiggling ever since, probably trying to get right side up—or in this case, right side down. Our Christmas miracle. She was so tiny when she was born and looked adorable tucked into the Christmas stocking we brought her home in. She and Lorena made the local news, they were airing a story about the stocking. When she cried for the first six months due to colic, we became desperate. Drives around the neighborhood, placed in her bouncy seat on the dryer, endless rocking in the chair. Nothing worked. It's true what they say: God gives you the easy one first so you'll have more. Alexis slept four hours the night we brought her home from the hospital; Ashlyn hasn't slowed down enough to sleep yet. She is a bundle of energy like her mom and excelled at soccer, flag football, and competitive cheerleading. She started out playing co-ed soccer with the boys, but after she wanted to invite only boys to her birthday party, Lorena and I decided she needed to join a girls' team. She went on to play competitive club soccer as well as high school soccer and flag football. She was also a cheerleader in ninth grade. In eleventh grade, she came home and announced she was going to be a pole vaulter. I reminded her that she'd never pole-vaulted before, and her response was classic Ashlyn: "I'll learn." And learn she did—she even qualified for States her senior year. She's never been afraid of anything and works very hard to achieve her goals.

Ashlyn also attended the University of Florida and is a huge Gator fan. She earned her degree in microbiology with a minor in medical geography and global health. She worked very hard and excelled in school. She will be attending medical school and has been working as a medical assistant, obtained a certificate in anatomy and physiology, and has nannied since graduating. She wants to be a pediatrician and loves children. She's been babysitting since she was old enough to take a baby CPR class, has worked as a camp counselor and medical intern at her camp in North Carolina, and wants to have four children. She often tells us that with all she wants to accomplish, she may die disappointed. I doubt that—she will achieve everything she sets her mind to.

Travel is another passion for Ashlyn. In the summer of 2023, she backpacked through Europe for two months and visited many of the great cities. She went alone, and although her mom and I were apprehensive, she did just fine. Once again, "fear" is not in her vocabulary, nor is "I can't." I wish I could bottle her energy and enthusiasm for life. Having Ashlyn home between UF and medical school has been a blessing. Before she returned from Italy in July 2023, Lorena and I decided it was finally time to get a new puppy. I had joked before leaving that I was tired of talking to the Roomba and wanted a dog. I should have known Lorena would jump on it. Within a week of my return, I was flying to northern Ohio to pick up Millie Mae, a tri-colored Cavachon (half King Charles Cavalier and half Bichon Frise). She's a great puppy but still full of energy. I had forgotten just how much energy puppies have, but Ashlyn keeps up with her every day and routinely wears her out.

### *Joseph Philip Ludovici Jr.*

In the spring of 2001, Lorena wasn't feeling well and went to the doctor to find out why. The doctor said, "You're not sick, you're pregnant." "WHAT? We don't just get pregnant," I said when she told me. It usually took a lot of money and medical treatment for us to conceive. Lorena had always wanted three children; I was content with our two girls and, after spending countless hours perfecting my Barbie and Bratz playing skills with Alexis and Ashlyn, I felt complete. Contrary to what people might think, we were not trying for a boy, but I have to admit I was thrilled when we saw the little "turtle" on the ultrasound at around twenty weeks. I'm sure my chest puffed out a bit more, and I strutted around for weeks. Joseph Philip Ludovici Jr. (JoJo) was born by cesarean on October 23, 2001—on his mom's birthday.

I had always loved my name as a kid. My parents told me I was the only child they knew who proudly told them they had given him the best name. I wasn't fond of "Joey" but loved "Joe." We doubled it and made it even better with "JoJo." He was named after JoJo Armington, whom I went to high school with and whom Lorena knew from UF. It was quite surprising when we realized we were both thinking of the same JoJo when we were deciding on a nickname.

Early on, we realized how easygoing and happy JoJo was. At about six months old, he needed surgery at All Children's Hospital in St. Pete. He had a growth under his tongue the size of a red-hot cherry ball (it was red in color and resembled a jawbreaker). Part of his thyroid hadn't descended properly, leaving him with this mass. While it wasn't believed to be cancerous or too serious, it did require surgery and general anesthesia, which was scary. The surgery went perfectly, according to the doctor. Within six hours, JoJo was up and out of bed, and by the next day, he was back to his usual happy self. You would never have known he'd had surgery the day before.

JoJo has always been an easygoing kid who loves sports and enjoys being part of a team. When he was three or four, we started him in soccer. He played alongside Derek Shaw, son of Bobby and Jerlyn; Aidan Bitter, son of Shelagh and Terry; and Christopher, son of Chris and Rene. It was awesome seeing JoJo playing with Derek as Bob and I had done when we were kids. I was the coach and devised a system using colored wristbands to help the kids stay in their positions—green for forward G - Go, yellow for L - left wing, red for R- right wing, and blue for defense, I just like the color blue. When I yelled for them to shoot the ball at the far post, Chris laughed, thinking it was too advanced for four-year-olds to understand. We won a lot of games, thanks to Aidan's amazing athleticism, Christopher's speed, and Derek's strong defense. JoJo was the consummate teammate and a great passer. At least he didn't tell me he didn't want me coaching him—whew! Aidan did once ask his parents, "Why is Coach Joe so different from Mr. Joe at church?" Admittedly, during football, I could be a bit over the top. Winning mattered to me –sometimes too much.

JoJo is also very smart. He earned straight A's in third grade and always said he wanted to be as smart as his big cousin Stephen—not a bad person to try to emulate academically. That year, after the first ten days of fall football practice, JoJo's coach told me that JoJo would be the starting quarterback. He said JoJo had great football smarts and showed me the roster with the GPAs of all the kids on the team. There were many A averages, but only one 100% score—JoJo's. He has a couple of nicknames: "Snubby" and "Smiley." Not the most intimidating for a football player, but it is what it is.

JoJo also enjoyed wrestling as a kid and won quite a few matches with his signature headlock and hip toss. But, like me, JoJo found wrestling to be a bit too intimate. He wasn't particularly fast (again, taking after his dad), so while soccer was fun, he was never going to be the next Messi. Then there was baseball. As I mentioned before, this was my favorite sport as a kid. JoJo played tee ball in first grade and did pretty well. He was a good fielder and could throw the ball from shortstop to first base on a line. The next year, he played coach-pitch baseball with Derek and Christopher, but he struggled. After the season, JoJo told me he didn't want to play baseball anymore. I was disappointed, but I knew it wasn't about me or my passion; it was about my son's passions. I wanted him to play a sport, but which one was up to him.

Football it was! JoJo played eight years of Pop Warner football with the Carrollwood Hurricanes alongside Aidan and Christopher. He played various positions, including center, and could execute a shotgun snap almost flawlessly. He even became the long snapper for his teams, which made me proud, as those were the positions I played. As he got older, however, his body type didn't quite fit the offensive line. Tall and lean like his grandfather Fred. Football was evolving from how it was played in the late 1970s, and smaller players weren't cut out for the offensive line. Tackle football was now played in both the fall and spring (8 v. 8), and JoJo enjoyed it. I coached and later became the football commissioner for the Carrollwood Hurricanes, but my favorite season was his last, when I wasn't coaching or acting as FC. I simply got to enjoy watching my son's games. Despite the Hurricanes' Orange and Green colors and nickname, which my dad loved seeing me wear as a devoted Gator fan, we had a great experience with Carrollwood.

In 2016, JoJo applied to and was admitted to Jesuit High School in Tampa, the most prestigious high school in the area. He did exceptionally well academically and played football all four years. He played defensive end and, although he was a bit light for the position, he stuck with it and became the team's hype man his senior year, responsible for firing up the team before they left the locker room. His senior year JoJo's team won the district and regionals and made it to states where they narrowly lost to Miami Northwestern, which went on to win the State Championship. JoJo made many close friends at Jesuit and, despite my initial reservations about him attending an all-male private Catholic school, as I had rejected in 9th grade, he loved it. When we asked him why he was so timely with his assignments in ninth grade compared to eighth grade (when we constantly had to remind him to submit his work), he said very flatly, "Because it matters now."

Despite his academic success and higher ACT scores than his sisters, JoJo did not get accepted to UF. We even had him retake the ACT, and when he scored higher, he reapplied. Again, he was not accepted. His mom and I were far more frustrated by this than he was. True to his easygoing nature, JoJo was happy to be accepted to FSU, and despite his sisters' relentless teasing about being a Nole, he found a great home there. He graduated Magna Cum Laude in 2024 with dual majors in real estate and finance and moved back to Tampa to start his career with Franklin Street, a commercial real estate brokerage firm. I expect that in the coming years, he will take on some responsibilities in managing the real estate holdings created by my dad and currently managed by my brother Ed and his daughter Christina. JoJo spent the summer of 2022 in Miami working with Ed and Christina. It fascinates me that while I ran away from this opportunity in real estate, JoJo seems to be running toward it.

I couldn't be prouder of the children Lorena and I have raised and look forward to all that they will experience in the years to come.

# Chapter 7

# The Challenge

*"Hello Joe, this is Dr. Fernandez's office we got the results back from your thallium stress test... you failed."*

*I retorted, "but I'm planning to fly to Vail tomorrow for a week of skiing."*

*She said, "well if you can come back to the office, get the catheterization done this afternoon/evening and if it is clean, you can fly out tomorrow."*

*I made a U-turn on the Courtney Campbell Causeway and headed back to Clearwater.*

*Dr. Fernandez's associate did the procedure through my wrist and despite the propofol I was awake during the procedure.*

*"So", I asked, "how's it looking?" the doc responded, "you're not going skiing tomorrow!"*

### *Something is Not Right*

In the fall of 1999, just before Ashlyn was born, I found myself in the middle of the most significant case of my career. The case revolved around proving that a claimant in a workers' compensation claim suffered from Munchausen's syndrome, a disorder where individuals intentionally cause harm to themselves to secure benefits they wouldn't otherwise receive. I had to travel frequently for depositions with medical experts in Sarasota, which was about an hour from the office and nearly two hours from home with traffic. After moving from Dana Shores to Odessa in northwest Hillsborough County in 1998, the commute to St. Petersburg had become even longer. Most depositions with doctors began around five o'clock, after office hours. And, as anyone familiar with doctor's offices knows, they are rarely punctual and even less eager to sit for depositions. As a result, the sessions often started late, and I wouldn't get home from Sarasota until well into the night. Over the course of the case, I conducted twenty-two depositions—an unusually high number for a workers' compensation case.

During this hectic period, I began noticing shortness of breath and a tightness in my chest when walking from the eleventh to the twelfth floor of our office building. Ashlyn was born in December, and I tried the case in January. Thankfully, I won; all benefits were denied. However, the physical symptoms persisted, and I also started experiencing personality changes. Anxiety crept into my daily life and I had a very hard time controlling my emotions. At Ashlyn's baptism in February, for example, I asked my brother, Ed, to keep an eye on Alexis as we crossed the grass parking lot of the church. Moments later, Alexis darted off, and panic set in.

With cars everywhere, I lost control, yelling at Ed and scolding Alexis in front of the entire family, scene I deeply regretted.

When I returned to work, I confided in my associate, Chris Petruccelli, about my symptoms. He shared that he'd experienced chest pains the previous year, which turned out to be acid reflux, and encouraged me to see his doctor. Assuming my symptoms stemmed from the stress of the case and sleepless nights with a newborn, I made an appointment with Dr. Ronald Vencencio in late February. I described my symptoms, which were inconsistent, and Dr. Vencencio performed an EKG to measure the electrical activity of my heart. The results weren't normal, and he referred me to a cardiologist. It was clear this wasn't acid reflux, but at that point, I wasn't overly concerned.

I made an appointment with Dr. Aland Fernandez, who took my medical history, repeated the EKG, and scheduled a thallium stress test. The test involved injecting nuclear thallium into my arteries, walking on a treadmill, and taking images of my heart. As I was driving home from Clearwater to Tampa on the Courtney Campbell Causeway, his office called me. The results indicated I needed an angiogram. An angiogram involves inserting a catheter into an artery and threading it up to the heart, where dye is injected to identify any blockages in the arteries supplying blood to the heart. At this point, I started to feel nervous. My cholesterol levels had always been high, and I had a family history of heart issues on both sides. My granny had died young from heart problems, my Nonno from heart failure, and my mom had undergone triple bypass surgery a few years earlier. But all of them were older—I was only thirty-six.

We were supposed to leave for a ski trip to Colorado the next day, so I pushed to have the angiogram done that evening, hoping for a clean result so I could still go. I turned around on the causeway and headed back to the hospital in Clearwater.

Meanwhile, Lorena was on Florida's east coast for depositions and had traveled there with one of her expert witnesses. Without a car to return quickly, her firm chartered a flight to the St. Petersburg/Clearwater airport so she could be with me before the procedure. Although I didn't expect them to find anything, I had to consent to an angioplasty and stents in case blockages were discovered. An angioplasty involves inflating a small balloon via the catheter to open the artery, followed by placing a stent—a wire mesh that keeps the artery from collapsing.

The procedure began around 7:00 p.m. While not under full anesthesia, I was sedated, leaving me foggy but still awake and able to talk. The oddest part was the injection of the dye, which caused a warm sensation to sweep through my body. Watching the dye move through my arteries on the monitor was fascinating, though the results were less so. It quickly became clear to everyone, including me, that skiing the next day was no longer an option.

I had a 95 percent blockage in my right coronary artery (RCA), requiring a stent, and a 90 percent blockage in my left anterior descending artery (LAD), ominously nicknamed the "widow maker," which also needed a stent. My doctors warned me that even if I had survived the flight to Colorado, I likely wouldn't have made it off the mountain in my condition. One doctor bluntly told me that if I wanted to walk my daughters down the aisle at their weddings, I needed to make significant lifestyle changes. Despite the gravity of the situation, I felt incredibly fortunate. My doctors had recognized the problem, pursued additional tests despite my atypical symptoms, and insisted I stay grounded until they were complete.

Unfortunately, my recovery wasn't smooth. By June 2000, I was back in the hospital with unexplained chest pain that baffled the doctors. This setback was frustrating, especially since I had tried to return to work but couldn't shake the feeling that something was still wrong. In April 2001, my RCA required re-stenting, prompting my doctors to recommend a less stressful occupation. The confidence I'd built throughout my legal career began to unravel. At the peak of my success, I was forced to pivot.

I still wanted to remain in the legal field, specifically workers' compensation, where I had built a strong network of friends and colleagues on both sides of the cases. To reduce my stress, I decided to become a Supreme Court Certified Circuit/Civil Mediator. Mediation involves assisting litigants in resolving disputes through guided negotiation. Although I had to give up my law firm partnership, I was fortunate that the group disability policy through my firm paid me benefits voluntarily. My private disability policy, which I had prudently purchased years earlier but never imagined needing, didn't accept my claim voluntarily. Ironically, I found myself litigating a disability case. After spending a decade defending such cases, I was now the claimant. We eventually settled, and that experience gave me a unique perspective to bring to mediation, blending the insights of a hard-nosed defense attorney with the empathy of a disability recipient. Mediation turned into a fulfilling career path, and I've since had the opportunity to teach negotiation and mediation classes at Stetson College of Law.

### *The Next Chapter*

Once I settled the group policy, I ventured into business. In 2003, I founded JAAC Enterprises (named after JoJo, Ashlyn, Alexis, and Chelsea). Chelsea was Ken Cooper's daughter; Ken was my fraternity brother from UF and a Disney employee at the time. He became my partner in the venture—I financed it, and he managed the day-to-day operations. Before purchasing the business, we hired an accountant to review the books and evaluate the company. Unfortunately, we ignored his expert advice. We were buying "a dinosaur," a domestic apparel manufacturing company, and he warned us it was a dying state side industry. Manufacturing was rapidly shifting overseas, leaving businesses like ours struggling to survive. Despite the red flags and our complete lack of experience in fashion, I went ahead and bought the company.

The prior owners had made some uniforms and costumes for Disney World, and with Ken's connections, we thought we could make it work. We took our shot and proposed a $4.5 million annual contract with Disney to manufacture all their uniforms and costumes for their theme parks. We went to Anaheim and made our pitch. Unfortunately, we did not get the contract. I couldn't afford to continue paying Ken his salary, and he returned to Disney, where he has done very well. I ran the business for a few more years until 2010, when I finally sold it at a loss. We never made money, and financially it was a disaster, but I appreciated the opportunity to see and feel something being made. As a bonus, my girls thought it was pretty cool that their Daddy made Cinderella and Snow White dresses, even though the contract with Disney prohibited us from making one for them. It was an expensive lesson to learn, but if you hire an expert, rely on their opinion!

### *Searching for Answers*

In a search for answers as to why I had such early onset of cardiovascular disease, I went to Johns Hopkins Hospital in Baltimore, Maryland. I saw an expert in early onset, and they ran a very specific test to determine not just the quantity of cholesterol but also the size. I knew I had high numbers of LDL (the bad cholesterol), but this test showed each molecule was also very small, which allows it to stick to the artery walls more easily. I also knew I had low numbers of HDL (the good cholesterol), but learned they were very large, which made it more difficult for them to absorb the bad cholesterol and carry it out of the blood. While this explained why I had the early onset of cardiovascular disease, it did not make me feel any better because there was nothing I could do with this information. I had to be on statins, reduce my stress, modify my diet to avoid saturated fats, and diligently do cardio exercises.

Unfortunately, my medical challenges were not over. In fact, they got far worse. In 2006, I was diagnosed with diabetes. Most diabetics are either Type 1 or Type 2. As usual, mine is a little more complicated than that. Like a Type 1 diabetic, my pancreas does not make sufficient amounts of insulin to combat the sugars. Like a Type 2 diabetic, my receptors in my cells do not properly receive the little bit of insulin I produce or the insulin that I inject. I also suffer from sleep apnea, which is an interruption of breathing during sleep. Additionally, I have two bad shoulders, which I have had operated on. I separated my right shoulder and had surgery in 1992, the same year I got married. I tell people I haven't had a good night's sleep since 1992, but I don't know whether it is from the marriage or the shoulder. Lorena doesn't like that joke. Recently, I separated my left shoulder skiing, which didn't help the chronic problem I have had with my left shoulder since surgery in 1993. Other orthopedic issues with my neck and back make getting a full night's sleep impossible. I have also had issues with concussions. I had two mild ones as a kid, and another in college which was so severe that I had three days of amnesia. Recently, after another couple of falls skiing, I had another concussion and subsequent headaches. Maybe it is time to give up skiing. I hope not.

### *The Big One*

As Fred Samford liked to claim when his son upset him he would clutch his chest and yell: *It's the big one, I'm comin' for you, 'lizabeth"* His was not a heart attack and neither was mine but it was a big one. In May of 2009, I was not feeling particularly well. I had continued with my semi-annual appointments with my cardiologist, Dr. Fernandez, and each year he ordered a thallium stress test that I had been passing regularly. Despite passing the test the previous November, I knew something was not right. I couldn't really explain it, but I just felt off. While at work at JAAC on May 19, 2009, I drove myself to the emergency room at Mease Countryside Hospital. They would not let me leave. They ordered a catheterization, but this time I received a lot of sedatives, and I don't remember the procedure. No angioplasties or stents were going to work this time. When I woke up, Dr. Fernandez told me I needed to consult with a surgeon for emergency bypass surgery. They transported me by ambulance to Morton Plant Hospital in downtown Clearwater, where I consulted with Dr. Heric, a thoracic surgeon and bypass specialist. He explained that I needed a quadruple bypass. The four major arteries supplying blood to my heart were barely functioning. The RCA was 99 percent blocked below the site of my previous stents, the LAD was 90 percent blocked, the left marginal (LM) was 70 percent blocked, and the circumflex marginal (CM) was 80 percent blocked. Amazingly, I hadn't had a heart attack, so my heart muscle was in great shape. I had surgery on May 21st.

I was in the hospital for five days after the surgery, which overlapped with the Memorial Day Weekend. Mike and Jackie Ortiz, our ski buddies, were the first to visit me on the day of the surgery. Somehow, they managed to get back to see me before Lorena had even been let in. Jay and Terry Hebert came to visit on their way to Ocala to spend Memorial Day with Jay's brother Randy's family on Lake Weir which had become our tradition.

Since law school, we had spent every Memorial Day with the Heberts, and it was a tradition I missed that year. Jay asked if Alexis could come with them to keep the tradition alive in a small way, and we, of course, said yes. Many friends visited me in the hospital, and some were visibly upset by how I looked. My mom, dad, and brother also came up for the surgery. The Kampsens, neighborhood friends who owned a condo on Clearwater Beach, let them stay there over the weekend. I gave my brother a hard time about me being in the hospital with tubes sticking out, while he enjoyed the beach. He and Dad don't handle medical situations well, but they were very supportive and great to have around the hospital... because it hurt like hell!

In order to work on your heart, they have to split your sternum and pull your chest open. When they tie you back up, they use what look like the steel ties we used to tie steel for pouring concrete footers like the ones we had used on the Rex and Mayfair buildings as kids. These still protrude from my chest, which is kind of gross. They also place tubes in your chest to drain the fluid (blood) from your chest cavity. I don't know if one of the tubes was rubbing against my spine or what, but not only was my chest hurting, my back was killing me while lying in the hospital bed. It did motivate me to get up and walk, which I did after three days, and I felt much better when they pulled out the tubes. It was funny, though—while Dr. Heric was talking to me, his very pretty and young physician assistant grabbed all three tubes and yanked them out without warning. If she hadn't been so pretty, I'm sure I would have punched her—it hurt so bad. While she was pulling out the tubes, Lorena yelled, "Oh my God!" She couldn't believe how long the tubes were. I told her afterward that she wasn't allowed to stay in the room if she was going to act like that when they did something to me. Fortunately, I got some relief from the back pain after they were removed.

When they discharge you, they send you home with some good pain medicine and a teddy bear. The idea is to hug the bear against your chest when you cough or move to help with the pain. I guess it helps a little, but not very much. Breathing hurt. Moving hurt. Coughing was miserable for weeks. My mom, my Florence Nightingale, stayed with us for two weeks, and with her, Lorena, Alexis, Ashlyn, and JoJo, I recovered pretty quickly. After eight weeks, I was able to drive myself again, which was a great relief. My neighborhood buddies Jack Kampsen, Fred Seguiti, and Steve Tenny were great about coming by and taking me out for lunch during that time. I don't think Lorena had to cook a meal for two months with all the food friends brought over. It was much rougher than I anticipated, but again, I felt fortunate that the doctors found and fixed the problems without me having a heart attack or significant damage to my heart muscle.

The surgery wasn't without complications. For the main two bypasses of the RCA and LAD, they were able to use my two mammary arteries. These bypasses should last forever since mammary arteries have a unique property: they don't acquire plaque or become blocked. Unfortunately, in July, I was back in the emergency room with severe chest pain. It was unlike anything I had felt before. Much worse that the pre or post op pain. The pain started around three in the morning, and when Lorena woke up at about seven, I told her I needed to go to the ER. I tend to downplay my concerns with her, and I must have done so that morning because when I went back into the bathroom to hurry her along, she was in the shower. I'm not very patient to begin with, and my patience was especially thin that morning.

Because the pain was so intense, we decided to go to the closest ER to our home, University Community Carrollwood. When we arrived, they told me based on my enzyme levels that I had had a heart attack. Since that hospital doesn't do interventions, they transferred me to the main hospital near USF—another ambulance ride. They performed an angiogram and found that the two arteries bypassed using arteries from my arm for the LM and CM had completely failed. They placed a stent in the LM, but because the CM was at a branch of the artery, they left it alone. I was discharged the next day, even though I was still complaining of severe pain.

That evening, we went to dinner at my in-laws' house. After talking with them, we decided to return to the ER—this time at Mease Countryside, where Dr. Fernandez is. Once again, they said I had, or was having, a heart attack. That night, Dr. Fernandez's associate performed another angiogram, placed two stents in the CM, and discovered that I had pericarditis. Pericarditis is inflammation of the sac around the heart. The inflammation causes the space between the heart and the sac to shrink, creating a sensation like scratching the side of a balloon with your finger. That awful screeching sound wasn't heard but was felt with pericarditis. The condition elevates enzyme levels and mimics a heart attack in blood tests. I hadn't had a heart attack, but it sure hurt like hell. They prescribed antibiotics, and I recovered from the pericarditis in a couple of weeks.

Unfortunately, the pericarditis returned in October, but by then, I had a pretty good idea of what it was. Once again, antibiotics worked, and I was okay within a few weeks. Pericarditis hurts worse than almost anything I've experienced, and the teddy bear didn't help at all.

### *Just a Little Something Else*

I say "almost anything" because I had one more trip to the ER and one more operation to endure. In January of 2011, JoJo and I were on our annual fishing trip to Orlando. Every year, Ken

205

Cooper charters a boat from Disney on Lake Buena Vista, and Benton Wood, his son Parker, JoJo, and I are his guests. Parker's birthday is in January, and he loves to fish. We fish in the morning, eat lunch, and then head to DisneyQuest. That year, we went to Blues Brothers Café, and I had a Reuben. As soon as lunch ended, the boys, Ken, and Benton headed into DQ to play games. I was feeling really bad and soon revisited my Reuben next to Cirque du Soleil. I was in tremendous pain and had no idea what it could be. I didn't think it was my heart, but I knew I wanted to get back to Tampa fast. I cut JoJo's trip to DQ short and got on I-4. Twice, we had to stop, and the pain and vomiting were bringing me to my knees on the side of the road. It must have been quite a sight. JoJo was worried and asked, "Are you okay, Daddy?" I wasn't sure. I called Lorena, and she called her mom. They finally met me near the Tampa Airport and drove us home.

When I got home, we immediately started the WebMD search. Lorena thought it was food poisoning because she'd had that several years before and it was miserable. The only issue was that food poisoning usually happens in multiple cases, and no one else was sick. I thought it could be appendicitis, but my pain was higher up in my stomach. I decided to try and get some rest and went to bed for the night. I rolled around most of the night, and at seven the next morning, I told Lorena the words I hate to utter: "I need to go to the ER." No shower for Lorena that morning. Because of the fiasco with the two ER trips and multiple doctors the year before, I had moved all my care to the new hospital near our home, St. Joseph's North. It is less than ten minutes from our house. Off to the ER we went!

Because of my cardiac history and the fact that there was no one else in the ER, I was seen right away. Once they determined it was unrelated to my heart, they ordered a sonogram and soon discovered that I had severe pancreatitis and gallstones. Apparently, a gallstone had settled in the duct of the pancreas and was blocking the site. The gallbladder was inflamed, which was causing all the pain. It was rare that I hadn't had any problems before Sunday morning, as most people suffer from gallbladder issues for years before surgery. They told me I would need surgery and would have to stay in the hospital until the infection settled down enough to safely perform it. I was in the hospital all week, lost about twenty pounds, and finally had the surgery on Friday.

It was supposed to be a quick recovery, done laparoscopically —two to three weeks, and everything would be fine. Instead, it took me three months before I started feeling better. I hadn't realized it before, but the gallbladder is a significant organ, and it takes the body time to adjust to having the liver regulate bile secretion directly instead of storing it in the gallbladder. The severe infection I experienced, coupled with the pericarditis from the year before (also an infection), was significant. Just after law school, my dentist diagnosed me with periodontal disease. I underwent two procedures to graft tissue from the roof of my mouth onto my gums, which had receded due to the disease. Coupled with the fact that heart disease is a type of inflammation—this time in the walls of the arteries—my doctors began to suspect something else might be going on.

I had seen an immunologist before the gallbladder issue, but we hadn't made much progress. Once I recovered, I was finally able to follow up with him, and he ordered additional blood work. It became clear that I had low immunoglobulin levels, the antibodies in the blood that fight infection. He recommended subcutaneous immunoglobulin injections, which I did for about six months. This required placing small needles in my stomach to infuse the missing immunoglobulin over two hours. These treatments were supposed to provide a boost that could last five to ten years and help me fight off infections.

### *6 Good Years*

I was following up with my new Cardiologist Dr. Pastore on a regular basis and was not having any issues. It was ten years since my bypass, but on July 29, 2015, I was working with Jay Hebert at his firm handling BP Oil Spill claims. Jay had a contractor buddy who was involved in a dispute with a customer. His deposition was scheduled, and despite my advice to keep his answers succinct, he seemed determined to turn it into a performance. During a break, I became extremely frustrated with his behavior and was screaming at him when I started experiencing chest pain. Jay suggested he could finish the deposition without me, so I went straight to St. Joseph's North ER. My new cardiologist, Dr. Pastore, performed an angiogram and stented the Distal LAD. I continued to have issues, and on December 16, 2015, the OM2 was also stented. Interestingly, even when I don't experience chest pain, I can usually tell when something is wrong by noticing changes in my temperament.

# Chapter 8

# Overcoming the Challenge...Sometimes

*"Stop cutting my tree!" I screamed at the young man over the roar of the chainsaw.*

*"You don't own the creek," he retorted.*

*"The hell I don't, I own to the center of the creek and all of these trees you see along here. " I...I was just trying to clear the path for the jet skis." he stammered.*

*"Before you decide to do me a favor, you should knock on my door and ask."*

*"The jet skis are the reason for all the erosion along the creek and why these beautiful Live Oaks are falling in the creek. Get the hell out of here and stay off my property." I grumbled.*

### *Nine Years This Time*

To say that I have "overcome" my medical challenges is a bit premature, but in 2023 I turned sixty—an accomplishment I do not take for granted. My latest issue with my heart was in 2024. We went to Calgary Banff and Jasper. When we arrived for our first hike I realized quickly that something was not right. I was having significant chest pain within the first 200 yards of a 3-mile hike.

Not happening. I told the girls and Lorena that I needed to turn back but that they should continue on the hike. They insisted that I call them every 15 minutes. I did. This was not even going to be the most difficult hike of the week and I was worried that I was going to ruin the "bucket list" item for Lorena.

Despite the pain, I made it through the week and did a lot with them except the hikes. Upon my return I decided to contact Dr. Pastore but unfortunately it was near the July 4th Holiday and he was out of the country, or at least the contiguous 48. He was in Hawaii with his family. I decided to head to the ER and I got quite a talking to from the nurses with Lorena nodding along, about not seeing someone in Canada when my symptoms started. I promised not to do that again. They contacted Dr. Pastore and scheduled me for a catheterization. Unfortunately, he was delayed on his return and Dr. Sai was called in to do the cath. But Dr. Pastore told me after that he would have likely called in Dr. Sai anyway because I was a "complicated case". Dr. Sai placed two stents on both sides of the stent placed by Dr, Pastore in 2015 on the OM2 and noted 99% blockage of the Diagonal artery but he did not stent it. On October 29, 2024, Dr. Sai attempted to stent the Diagonal artery but was unable to because it was 100% blocked by then and had started to atrophy distally.

I will be heading for another opinion with a Dr. Chris White at the Ochsner Clinic in New Orleans. Stay tuned…

## Why I am Who I Am                    Joseph P. Ludovici

While my confidence has waned, I still have hints of that CONFIDENCE I carried years ago. Life has a way of sapping your confidence, but traces of it remain. Once, while refueling my car with JoJo, we saw two teenagers beating up another boy. Without thinking, I stepped in and broke up the fight. Probably not the smartest move, especially with my son right there, but I have always confronted injustice when I thought it was the right thing to do. I remember sitting in a partner's meeting at Fox and Grove, where Bob Byelick was being unfairly attacked by another partner. I jumped in to defend Bob, and it probably cost me. I didn't care because it was the right thing to do. Lorena always told me not to be the lightning rod, but I never took that advice well.

It may be a genetic thing. I was not intimidated by the challenge of going against Lomas Brown in football or beating Southridge in baseball. In college, I was confronted by about fifty Auburn students who took my Gator hat and burned it. I had eight fraternity brothers with me, and I figured those were decent odds. I didn't back down. At a softball tournament, I got into a confrontation with a first baseman who was six foot five. While it was more head-to-chest than chest-to-chest, again, I wouldn't back down. The Gators play Tom Petty's "I Won't Back Down" at the end of the third quarter, and I guess that's been my motto long before the song became a tradition at Gator games.

Unfortunately, I have passed that trait on to my kids, especially Ashlyn. At a Lightning game, two Bruins fans sitting behind us were being very rude and making crude comments about women's body parts. Ashlyn, who was only a senior in high school at the time, turned around and confronted them. She jumped right in, standing up to these two grown men. While it was the right thing to do, I had to tell her afterward that sometimes it's better to ignore certain things and be more prudent. She disagreed as I probably would have at her age.

Recently, I got "way too worked up," as Lorena put it, about teenaged boys speeding dangerously through our creek on jet skis after dark. Not only were they being unsafe, but they were also causing harm to our property. I had undertaken a massive effort to stop the creek from eroding our yard, and their wake was reversing all that work. Stress, anxiety, anger—all of these are not good for heart disease, but I struggle to control them. This is my greatest challenge. It's not always the physical challenges you have to overcome, but the mental and emotional ones as well.

Most men identify themselves by what they do. When I could no longer be a trial attorney, I struggled with my identity. Fortunately, I worked with a couple of good therapists over the years and learned a lot about how to view one's self-worth. Being there for my children and being the best Dad I could be was much more important that being a trial lawyer.

Turning sixty is an accomplishment and a milestone I wanted to mark with significance. My close friends and fraternity brothers, Benton Wood and Dave Henley, have also faced serious heart issues in the last ten years, and we have often spoken about how making it to sixty is a remarkable achievement for all of us. For Benton, he survived a ruptured aorta—a condition that is rarely seen or successfully treated and Dave who "died" at the end of a 10k race but fortunately collapsed at the end of the race where the medical team was and they successfully resuscitated him.

### *A Trip of a Lifetime*

To mark this "accomplishment," I decided to give myself a big birthday gift: spending three months in Italy in the late spring and early summer of 2023. The goal was to connect with my Italian heritage, live like an Italian in small towns, visit with family, and research my Ludovici and Paone roots. Oh, and finally finish this book, which has taken me fifteen years to write. It was also an opportunity to reflect on the stories I've shared and appreciate the many good fortunes I've experienced over the past sixty years.

The first three weeks of my trip were spent just outside the town of Putignano, Bari, Puglia. Putignano is a typical medieval town, surrounded by a wall with a road outlining it. I stayed in a Trullo, a mortar-less, cone-shaped stone home that dates back to the fifteenth century. These homes were built as "temporary" shelters for farm workers, designed to be easily deconstructed when the King's tax man came to collect from landlords, saving them on taxes. Lorena and Ashlyn joined me in the Trullo for the first week of my stay. It was a little cold in Putignano, and we quickly learned that the Trullo's thick stone walls retained the chill even when the sun came out.

We found a fantastic restaurant that truly captured the spirit of southern Italy: Ristorante Chi Va Piano, or "who goes slowly." Their trademark is a turtle. I also loved Friggitoria San Domenico, where I enjoyed the octopus salad and clams with linguini. I ate there three times, and their octopus salad was the best I had in all of Puglia.

I visited at least twenty small medieval towns, from Bari on the east coast to Taranto on the west coast, most of which have large residential areas surrounding them. The residential areas are UGLY. They all share the same style: square buildings four to five stories high with plain, square balconies. As far as I can tell, there was one architect and one builder responsible for all of them across Italy. There are no suburbs as we know them—no quarter- or half-acre plots outside of town where kids play in the streets until the streetlights come on. Outside the towns, the countryside stretches for miles with acres of farms dotted with Trulli and small farmhouses. Occasionally, I came across a large villa or estate, which I would stop to explore. Most have been converted into wedding or event venues. I didn't experience agritourism, which has become very popular, but it's on my list for next time.

The countryside was full of olive trees, and I visited an EVOO (extra virgin olive oil) factory. Making olive oil is a pretty simple process, but since the harvest takes place in October and November, I only got to taste the final product. I learned that the pits aren't removed from the olives before they're manually crushed and squeezed. The first press produces "extra virgin" oil, and this factory sold its leftover mash to other companies to make non-virgin oil using a chemical extraction process.

Cherries were in season, and acres of these sweet treats were everywhere—one of my favorites. Fresh artichokes were also plentiful, and I tried them prepared in several ways. My favorite was pan-seared. Delizioso! In Bari, I watched two women making Orecchiette pasta. Orecchiette, which means "tiny ears" in Italian, is shaped by rolling small pieces of dough with their fingers into cupped, ear-like shapes. Their speed was incredible to watch. I bought some and made my own sauce with EVOO, garlic, spices, olives, and artichokes. Pretty darn good with a glass of local wine from the Negroamaro grape.

I attended my first professional futbol' game between Bari and Reggiana. What an experience—the fans in the end zones never stop chanting, singing, and cheering. The seaside towns were stunning, and the water of the Adriatic was beautiful. The beaches, however, were mostly rocky with little sand. Being from Florida, I couldn't help but compare them to our west coast beaches with their white sugar sand, which are much more beautiful—and comfortable.

Puglia's geography is diverse, stretching from the sea to the mountains. The people were friendly and accommodating. I often ate at off times, which is easy in Italy because dinner is served so late. When restaurants weren't too busy, the staff would let me practice my Italian with them. My experience in Puglia was fantastic, and I'm very glad I started my journey there.

My stay in Barete, L'Aquila, Abruzzo, was everything I could have hoped for. It was just a short drive to Cagnano Amiterno and Fiugni, and it delivered information that was critical in completing this book. I visited five cemeteries in and around the area and found many Ludovicis, Paones, and Paonis. Fortunately, none of them were alive—now that would have been a bit scary in a cemetery. After three days, my cousin Pino Di Loretto arrived from Rome. I must have been complaining to Pino because when he arrived, he said, "So you want to meet living Paone family?" I said, "Yes, of course," and he replied, "Let's go."

We packed my things, and within five minutes of leaving my Airbnb, we were standing at Sante Rocchi's feed store, just off the highway from Barete to Fiugni. Pino knew of these folks from his childhood when he would visit with his Nonna—my Zia Eva—to buy supplies during his summer stays in Fiugni. Zia Eva was very gregarious and well-known in the area.

We met who I called "the Queen," Jolanda Marimpietri Rocchi, Sante's mom and the daughter of Gilda Paone Marimpietri, my Nonna's sister. Jolanda is ninety-eight years old, and I absolutely adore her. Sante's wife, Gabriella, was fantastic, and once she figured out how to use Google Translate, we communicated fantastically. Their two daughters, Loreta and Emanuela, were incredibly helpful. They welcomed me into their home for Sunday dinner that week, serving a four-course meal plus dessert. The girls spoke some English and enjoyed practicing with me. I invited them to visit us in Florida, and hopefully, they will.

Loreta and Emanuela arranged a visit to Fiugni with Marisa and Nello. Marisa grew up in Fiugni and showed me where Benedetto Paone's, my Biznonno's (great grandfather in Italian) house was. The initials "BP" were still visible above the old door. My Nonna was raised in this house. We also met Benedetta Di Mario, a ninety-year-old lifelong resident of Fiugni, who shared an interesting story: the sons of Benedetto—Stefano, Adamo, and Filipo—began construction of a new house, which they called "the colosseum," at the turn of the 20th century. I shared the story of the 36-cod fish earlier in this book and the disagreement that left the house unfinished. According to Maria, Stefano would go out every morning to the clearing next to the colosseum, look down on the town of Fiugni, and say his prayers before reentering the BP house for his morning coffee. It really is a fantastic view.

Benedetta also talked about Amalio Paone, how handsome he was, and how well off he seemed to be. Amalio lived just two doors down from her and next door to her daughter, Pasqualina. His house is for sale, and Benedetta even gave me the contact information for the owner. She really wanted me to buy the house so we could be neighbors. You never know. I seem to have a way with ninety-year-old Italian women.

With Pino and sometimes on my own, I made several visits to the public records office in Cagnano Amiterno. We searched through birth and marriage records and found both of my grandparents' birth certificates, along with several others of interest. On Pino's last day with me, we sat in front of the Chiesa dei Santi Cosma e Damiano, waiting for the office to open, and talked about our findings. We remembered wanting to view the church records from Fiugni, but the recent earthquakes had hit the church hard, and the records book had been removed. Pino remembered Father Don Vito, and after a brief search we found him. He was dressed as if heading off for a construction job. He looked nothing like a Catholic priest. His hands were calloused and leathery. We asked about the marriage book from 1928, and he quickly returned with it and offered it to us as he had to hurry away to a prior engagement. We quickly found my Nonni's marriage certificate with the unusual Archbishops stamp on it.

This was significant because it confirmed that they were married in Fiugni and had not eloped to marry despite the protests of Stefano Paone, my Nonna's brother. Stefano had refused to sign a civil marriage record in Cagnano Amiterno, where he, as podesta, would have had authority. In 1932, someone submitted the marriage certificate to the archbishop of L'Aquila, and his stamp is on the document. Interestingly, most other certificates in the book do not have the archbishop's stamp. Was this some type of confirmation of the wedding between my Nonni that someone wanted to have validated? I don't know but it certainly was a rare find.

Unfortunately, my stay in Barete was interrupted due to my mom's serious medical condition and hospitalization in Miami. After my first week in Barete, I decided I needed to be with her. I had spoken to her every day while she was in the hospital, but on my last day in Barete, she told my brother she didn't want to speak with me. That was when I decided to return to Florida. Lorena made all my flight arrangements, and the following day I was on my way to Rome to fly to Miami. I take full credit for my mom's remarkable recovery. We kept it a secret that I was coming home because she would have objected, but when I saw her, she was overjoyed. She rapidly improved, and after a few more days in the hospital, she was discharged home.

I spent the next couple of days with her at home, and when I was convinced she was truly on the mend, I decided I could return to Italy. I'm so thankful I did because my return trip produced my Nonna's birth certificate, which we had missed on our first visit, and the marriage certificate for my Nonni. I can't thank Pino and the Rocchi family enough for the information they shared and the time they spent helping me with my research while also welcoming me as family.

My last three weeks in Italy were dedicated to rest and relaxation. Lorena and Alexis joined me in Bevagna, Perugia, Umbria. Bevagna is a walled city in southern Umbria, just north of Abruzzo. My Airbnb was just inside the Gaite Cannara, leading north out of the town. When I arrived, I found myself in the middle of the town's biggest festival, Il Mercato delle Gaite. This medieval festival features townspeople dressed in period clothing celebrating the four medieval gates of the city. Merchants, leather workers, blacksmiths, paper and bookmakers, and animal handlers displayed and sold their wares. The festival concluded with an archery competition where competitors represented each of the four gates. Townspeople cheered for their gate's archer whenever they broke a ceramic plate. When Lorena and Alexis arrived, we hiked to waterfalls, attended a wine tasting, visited Spoleto for an arts festival, saw a dance performance, participated in a truffle hunt, and took a cooking class. These amazing experiences brought my trip to a fantastic conclusion.

# Chapter 9

# My Next Thirty Years

*"Dad how are you doing?" I asked.*

*Which I already knew was not good. He had spent the night before I arrived, grabbing at his IVs and oxygen mast. But as I sat there with his arms restrained, I knew it was not going to be long.*

*In one of the most lucid and relaxed moments for the several days I was there, he motioned for me to come close and I lifted his mask so he could speak more easily.*

*"What are we doing all this for?" He whispered. "I've had a long life and I've accomplished all that I could..."*

*"I understand Dad, don't worry about Mom, Ed and I will take care of her, you can rest."*

### Two Examples to Learn from

Tim McGraw sang the country song "My Next Thirty Years" about how his life was going to be in the second thirty years and how it would differ from his first thirty years. Well, of course no one knows what the future holds but I will tell you what I want out of my next thirty years. As I said before, I am grateful for my second thirty and looking forward to the years to come, however many there will be.

I have learned something: difficulty does not end. I remember thinking that if I could just get the kids out of diapers, things would be so easy. Then thinking, how happy I was to get them all out of elementary school finally. I thought those were tough issues, but I learned the bigger the kids are, the bigger the issues are. Granted, there are fewer, but when they come, some are really hard. Once you get your kids graduated from high school and college, whew, you are empty nesters. Unfortunately, that is about the time your parents' health starts to be a challenge. We lost my Dad in 2017 and my father-in-law, Fred, in 2020 after a brutal three-year struggle with pancreatic cancer. These two men were important influences at two different times in my life as to why I am who I am today.

I don't know what challenges I will face, but I am certain there will be some. I hope I can face them with the same strength and dignity I learned from my Dad and Fred. I went to Miami to visit my Dad just before he died. In the hospital, at one point, he looked at me and with a very lucid and clear mind asked, "What are we doing all this for?"

At that point, he had been in the hospital for about two weeks, and he knew he was not going to be leaving. He knew he had lived a full life (almost eighty-eight years) and that he had accomplished all that he could. He was tired of being poked and prodded by the doctors and nurses and just wanted peace. When he was not in his right mind, he had been tearing at his IVs and the breathing mask they had on him. Again, he just wanted to be at peace. We decided as a family that we would place him in hospice, which I never really understood. You can be in hospice at the hospital. The care just shifts from providing remedial care to making the patient comfortable. This was what we knew he wanted, and within a few hours of hospice being called in and morphine being administered, he passed very peacefully.

The other side of the coin was Fred. He was diagnosed with Pancreatic cancer. He was still relatively young (seventy-five) when he was diagnosed, and he wanted to fight. He went to Philadelphia and had a very complicated surgery by one of the top pancreatic surgeons in the world. This brought him about eighteen months of relative comfort. But unfortunately, the cancer returned and metastasized. He still wanted to continue the fight.

This time, he had surgery in Tampa, and unfortunately, he never really improved. He continued to lose weight, and eventually, he withered away and died. I was so proud of JoJo the night before Fred died because he caringly lifted his grandfather from his bed to the hospital bed we had moved into the house that day. Ashlyn did not shy away from cleaning up the bile and vomit Fred was experiencing, and it reminded me of doing the same for my Nonna so many years before. Alexis was also able to be there since she was back home during the pandemic. She lovingly spoke to her grandfather to comfort him.

I know having all his grandkids with him was a great comfort to Fred. Fred told Mary a few days before he died that he had seen Jesus. He was comforted by the fact that his mother and father were waiting for him in heaven.  It was remarkable the night before he died that Lorena was asking him about the experience and he insisted that is was not a dream and that he had seen them. She was asking Fred follow-up questions about what and who he had seen.  He responded, "we make it too complicated".  This gave them peace and peace is an important step towards death for both the dying and those left behind.

Neither of these ways is the "right" way. Everyone has to make their own decision on what they want to do and how they want to pass. I don't know what my decision will be, but I hope that I will go peacefully in my sleep, the benefit of heart disease over cancer. It does not allow your family to say goodbye, which is hard for them, but in my experience, it is much easier for the patient. I'm thinking of my Uncle Bob and my buddy Steve, who we did not get to say goodbye to but who also did not suffer. They simply went to sleep and did not wake up, just like my Granny. I hope I find the elusive peace before I pass.

## *Plenty Left TO DO*

I also expect there to be many joyful and wonderful experiences. I think Lorena and I will have many vacations that we will enjoy and that she will continue to plan our lives as well as she has done for the last thirty years. She WILL NOT let grass grow under our feet. I hope we will get a second home built in North Carolina to replace the cabin we owned with my in-laws (the new cottage is in the works). That cabin was my happy place, where I enjoyed the cooler springs, summers, and falls. Having lived in Florida my whole life, I never experienced the change of seasons. I never acclimated to the heat in Florida (getting used to the heat is a myth). I think six months in the mountains and six months in Tampa would be ideal. A lot will depend on where our children and, hopefully, grandchildren end up. That road map has not yet been printed.

We were very fortunate when we moved from Dana Shores to Odessa: we developed some really great friendships. These came about when Lorena met Mary Seguiti and Catherine Cherniak at Alexis' preschool at Van Dyke United Methodist Church. Casey was in Alexis' class and Mary and Fred lived just across the street from the church. They soon moved into their new house around the corner from our home(s) on Hutchison Road, and Mary invited Lorena to a Bunco group in Van Dyke Farms. We met Catherine and Mike Cherniak, Lee and Jack Kampsen, Alicia and Steve

Tenny, Gabby and Frank Aguilar, Chuck, and Karen O'Neil, and Catherine and Mike Beam.

Our next set of friends was from Ashlyn's age group: Sylvia and Hark Harrison, Rob and Anna Ryan, Marge and Ben Bennett, Leslie and Scott Winterberg (who were also our best tenants ever in the grey house for four years), and others from the PTA. We also made great friends at JoJo's preschool and Wednesday night church, Shelagh and Terry Bitter. Their son Aidan and JoJo were best buddies in preschool and stayed friends playing Pop Warner football together for many years. Even though they went to separate high schools and colleges, they have stayed close playing video games online. We made many other great friends at Van Dyke, including Jackie and Mike Ortiz, who became our great ski friends at Snowmass every spring break.

Life is unpredictable, and there will be many turns in my path, but I am grateful for the experiences I have had and for the friends and family who have supported me and helped me along the way. I am also thankful for my children and the legacy I will leave through them. They have each accomplished so much already, and I could not be prouder to be their Dad. I hope they have learned some things from me, both what to do and what not to do. I believe that God has a plan for my life that, to be honest, I could not have imagined forty years ago, but I am fortunate to have lived the life I have and to have the opportunity to live some more of it. I am the product of the American Dream and through hard work, perseverance, and determination, that American Dream is still alive and well for the next generations. From my grandparents who took big risks and moved their families for a better opportunity, to my parents who, through education, accomplished the American Dream, to the legacy Lorena and I will leave to our children, the gifts with which we have been entrusted have served us well. For that, I am eternally grateful.

# Epilogue

Most people say that writing can be a cathartic experience. While part of this journey may have been therapeutic, a lot of it was nerve-racking. Putting oneself out there in the public domain is not easy. I have shared the stories I have shared here with family and friends and some of them I did not have right. I tried to correct them the best I could, but while I'll never be considered to have the memory of an elephant, these are my stories. Any remaining inaccuracies are my fault and if I got it wrong, I apologize.

Made in the USA
Coppell, TX
12 February 2025

45842251R00138